DECORATIVE PRINTED
MAPS
OF THE 15th TO 18th CENTURIES

DECORATIVE PRINTED

MAPS

OF THE 15th TO 18th CENTURIES

A revised edition of

OLD DECORATIVE MAPS AND CHARTS

by A. L. Humphreys

With eighty-four reproductions
and a new text by

R. A. SKELTON, F.S.A.

Superintendent of the Map Room, British Museum

SPRING BOOKS • LONDON

FIRST PUBLISHED 1952
Copyright 1952 R.A. Skelton

This edition published 1965 by
Spring Books
Drury House · Russell Street · London WC2

Second Impression 1966

Printed in Great Britain by
Richard Clay (The Chaucer Press) Ltd, Bungay, Suffolk

Contents

List of Plates

(those in colour are indicated by an asterisk)

Preface

THE CHANGE in the form of this book calls for some explanation. The first edition, compiled by the late A. L. Humphreys and published in 1926, was designed as a picture book to illustrate the wealth of a notable collection. Humphreys, a connoisseur of fine books, was impressed by the decorative beauty of the maps in early atlases, and selected his reproductions to excite the curiosity of collectors. Although his book made its contribution to the modern vogue for early maps, its text was discursive in form and did not attempt to provide the precise and detailed information which is to-day expected by those interested in early cartography.

The new edition is intended to serve both as a specimen book and as an elementary guide to the study of maps printed from wood blocks or copper-plates between the 15th and the 18th centuries: that is, from the birth of map-printing to the eve of modern scientific cartography. The Introduction gives a systematic account of the processes by which maps were, in this period, drawn, decorated, reproduced, and published. The treatment of these topics is deliberately simple (not, it is hoped, at the expense of correct perspective) and attempts to answer many questions which are commonly put to the present writer in the course of his professional work. While neither the text nor the choice of plates illustrates, except by implication, the growth of geographical knowledge or the history of instrumental survey, the technical aspects of map-printing have exercised a significant influence on the diffusion of geographical ideas which cannot be ignored by historically-minded geographers.

The majority of the plates in the first edition have been retained, and twenty-two new illustrations have been introduced by the present editor. Manuscript maps are still unrepresented. The plates have been re-arranged, and the new text has been written as a companion to them. Each of the eight chapters following the introduction and general bibliography deals with one group of plates and comprises a short historical essay, a select bibliography, and notes on the plates. In the text and in the choice of new illustrations more conspicuous notice has been given to English maps, which may be expected to have special interest for English-speaking readers.

The plates taken over from the first edition are reproduced from maps in the Macpherson Collection, now in the National Maritime Museum. The originals of the new plates (1, 3b, 10b, 11, 12, 31, 32, 34–36, 41, 42, 53, 61, 65, 68–70, 80–82, 84) are in the British Museum. The Trustees of these Museums have kindly given their permission for reproduction.

R. A. S.

Tilford, Surrey, 1952

The opportunity of reprinting has been taken to make a few minor corrections in the text, and to add a list of some of the more important works published since 1952. These are cited in the Bibliographical Note on the next page.

November 1964

R. A. S.

Bibliographical Note (1965)

Since 1952 the literature on the history of cartography has been enriched by a number of important works. Full lists are given in the bibliographies in the annual volumes of *Imago Mundi*. A few outstanding works, supplementing the bibliographies in the present volume, are mentioned below.

General bibliography (pp. 29-33)
G. R. Crone, *Maps and their makers* (2nd ed., 1962) is the best single-volume history of cartography in English. L. Bagrow's *Geschichte* is now available in an English edition, *History of cartography* (1964). Two valuable guides to map-collections and their holdings, in the Netherlands and Poland respectively, have appeared: C. Koeman, *Collections of maps and atlases in the Netherlands* (1961), and M. Lodyński, *Centralny katalog zbiorów kartograficznych w Polsce* (1961-63).

Two encyclopaedic facsimile atlases, although mainly concerned with manuscript maps, must be cited: Prince Youssouf Kamal, *Monumenta cartographica Africae et Aegypti* (1926-51), and A. Cortesão (with A. Teixeira da Mota), *Portugaliae monumenta cartographica* (1960-62). In the series *Theatrum orbis terrarum*, publication of which began in 1963, a large number of important early atlases are being made available in facsimile. Many of the older, and now scarce, reference books cited in the bibliographies have recently been reprinted by offset lithography.

Among recent works on regional cartography, the following deserve mention: for Italy, R. Almagià, *Documenti cartografici dello Stato Pontificio* (1960); for Germany, W. Bonacker, *Grundriss der fränkischen Kartographie des 16. und 17. Jahrhunderts* (1959), and other works by this author; for Switzerland, W. Blumer, *Bibliographie der Gesamtkarten der Schweiz . . . bis 1802* (1957); for France, F. de Dainville, *Cartes anciennes de l'Eglise de France* (1959) and *Le langage des géographes* (1964); for the British Isles, E. M. Rodger, *The large scale county maps of the British Isles 1596-1800: a union list* (1960), and J. H. Andrews, *Ireland in maps* (1961; with a 'bibliographical retrospect', 1962); and for America, F. Vindel, *Mapas de América en los libros españoles de los siglos XVI al XVII* (1955-59) and W. P. Cumming, *The south-east in early maps* (1958). Further references can be found in the classified bibliography in Bagrow's *History of cartography* (1964).

Chapters I—VIII
A few additions to the bibliographies of these chapters are listed below.
Chapter I (pp. 36-7)
  W. H. Stahl, *Ptolemy's Geography: a select bibliography* (1953).
Chapter II (p. 39)
  F. van Ortroy, *Bibliographie de l'oeuvre de Pierre Apian* (1901).
Chapter IV (p. 48)
  B. van't Hoff, *Jacob van Deventer* (1953).
  M. van Durme, *Correspondence mercatorienne* (1959).
  'Gerhard Mercator (1512-94) zum 450. Geburtstag', in *Duisburger Forschungen*, VI (1962).
  J. Keuning, 'The Van Langren family', in *Imago Mundi*, XIII (1956).
  J. Keuning, 'The "Civitates" of Braun and Hogenberg', in *Imago Mundi*, XVII (1963).
Chapter V (p. 56)
  E. M. Rodger, *The large scale county maps of the British Isles, 1596-1850: a union list* (1960).
  G. R. Crone, E. M. J. Campbell, R. A. Skelton, 'Landmarks in British cartography', in *Geographical Journal*, CXXVIII (1962).
  R. A. Skelton, *County atlases of the British Isles, 1579-1850* (1964; in progress).
Chapter VI (pp. 62-3)
  J. Keuning, 'Pieter van den Keere, 1571-1946 (?)', in *Imago Mundi*, XV (1960).
  J. Keuning, 'Blaeu's Atlas', in *Imago Mundi*, XIV (1959).
  C. Koeman, 'Some new contributions to the knowledge of Blaeu's atlases', in *Tijdschr. v. h. Kon. Ned. Aardr. Gen.*, LXXVII (1960).
  C. Koeman, *Collections of maps and atlases in the Netherlands* (1961).
Chapter VIII (pp. 74-5)
  A. H. W. Robinson, *Marine cartography in Britain* (1962).

Introduction

I. THE MAP AS A WORK OF ART

A MAP IS A GRAPHIC DOCUMENT in which location, extent, and direction can be more precisely defined than by the written word; and its construction is a mathematical process strictly controlled by measurement and calculation. The completed map must nevertheless be drawn by the hand of the cartographer. This is a freehand process in which the individual style of the draughtsman may be perceived. The map-maker, working within a narrower convention, has less scope for idiosyncracy than (for instance) the landscape artist; yet his hand may be betrayed by such formal qualities as lettering and ornament, which are sometimes in fact more reliable, as clues to the authorship and date of a map, than its geographical content.

This is more plainly seen in maps drawn before the period of accurate survey than in the relatively impersonal modern map. Until the 18th century, the map-maker was handicapped by many deficiencies of knowledge and technique: his surveying methods and instruments developed slowly from crude and inaccurate prototypes, units of measurement were not standardised nor correctly related to the size of the earth, he could not determine longitude with any certainty, magnetic variation was imperfectly understood, and (not least compelling) printed maps had to find a patron or a market. But, if these constraints reduced the scientific usefulness of his map, they offered the cartographer a larger field in which to exercise his sense of fitness in design and pattern, his ingenuity in ornament, and even his fancy. As Swift satirically wrote:

> So geographers, in Afric maps,
> With savage pictures fill their gaps,
> And, o'er inhabitable downs,
> Place elephants for want of towns.

That the craftsman's delight in decorating the face of his maps was not 'cabin'd, crib'd, confin'd' by the printing process, is made plain by the reproductions in this book, which are limited to printed maps.

'Geographie', wrote William Cuningham in 1559, quoting Ptolemy on maps, 'is the imitation, and description of the face, and picture of th' earth'; and maps are made primarily to furnish topographic information to practical men – seamen and travellers, soldiers and statesmen and scientists. They may also be a source of visual pleasure, objects to charm the sense of such as Georg Braun, 'drawne by a naturall love of Pictures and Mappes, Prospective and Chorographical delights', or as Thomas Hobbes who 'when at Oxford . . . used to love to visit the bookseller's shops, there to lye gaping on maps'.[1] Of the collectors of his day Dr John Dee wrote in 1570: 'Some, to beautify their Halls, Parlors, Chambers, Galeries, Studies, or Libraries with . . . liketh, loveth, getteth, and useth, Maps, Charts, and Geographicall Globes'. To such amateurs of maps the present book is addressed. The later sections of this Introduction consider the decorative printed map as a work of art, and the conditions in which it was drawn, reproduced, diffused and collected from the 15th to the 18th centuries.

---

[1] Both these quotations are from 17th-century writers. To Robert Burton is due the reference to Braun, and to John Aubrey the anecdote about Hobbes.

For the reproduction and multiplication of the hand-drawn map different engraving techniques have been used. The history of their application to cartography shows a continuous search for the most flexible process, that which will reproduce the draughtsman's line most sensitively and accurately.

These processes fall into three groups, distinguished by their technique and the material used:

(1) *Relief* processes, in which the design to be inked is left in relief, the unprinted portions being cut away from the surface of the wood-block or metal plate.

(2) *Intaglio* processes, in which the design is cut on a metal plate by a graving tool (as in line-engraving) or eaten away by acid (as in etching). The plate is inked, wiped, and passed through the press with a sheet of damped paper, which draws up the ink retained in the incised lines of the metal.

(3) *Surface* processes, in which the design is drawn (not cut) on a specially prepared surface, e.g. that of a lithographic stone. These processes were not used for maps before the 19th century and will not concern us here.

In all these techniques the design is drawn in reverse on the plate or block.

Both the woodcut (a relief process) and copper-plate engraving (an intaglio process) were from the earliest period used for the printing of maps. The woodcut started with some initial advantages which made it more popular with map-makers of the 15th and early 16th centuries. It had a longer history of trial and experience behind it when the first maps were printed; and until about 1550 the centres of geographical science in Central Europe were those cities (Nuremberg, Augsburg, Strassburg, Basle) where wood-engraving most flourished. To take impressions from the inked relief surface of a wood-block requires much less pressure, and so a simpler type of press, than printing from a copper plate, into the engraved lines of which the paper must be forced. Above all, both the wood-block and the movable type for letterpress had their printing surfaces in relief; they could be fitted together into the printer's 'forme' and the map (or illustration) printed in the same operation as the text. Far the greater number of 15th-century maps, from the earliest in 1472, were published in books, and if we remember that the use of illustrations from copper plates compelled the printer to put his sheets through the press a second time, we shall understand why copper-plate engraving only established its ascendancy as a medium for map reproduction when sheet maps came into vogue in the 16th century.

For similar reasons, the first printed maps did not appear until nearly three decades after the introduction (about 1440–50) of movable types for book printing, although wood-engraving had already been practised from about 1400 and printing from metal plates for almost as long. The earliest printed maps were copies from those in manuscripts of the geographical manuals of the late Middle Ages (Isidore of Seville, Pomponius Mela, Macrobius, Ptolemy), and so made their appearance in the printed editions of these works. In this as in other ways, the early printed book took the manuscript as its prototype.

Apart from the maps in the editions of Ptolemy printed at Bologna in 1477, at Rome in 1478 (reprinted in 1490, 1507 and 1508), and at Florence in 1482, and the map of Central Europe (1491) ascribed to Cardinal Nicholas of Cusa, no important maps were engraved on copper in the 15th century. The predominance of the woodcut as a medium for map printing continued until nearly the middle of the 16th century, and in Central Europe longer still. The revival and triumph of copper-plate engraving are described in Chapters III and IV (pp. 42–50 below). Its success and continued employment for over three centuries (and indeed until to-day) were due to its inherent fitness as a vehicle for the linear handiwork of the map-draughtsman. With little or no loss of style, the lightly incised line reproduced the outlines traced by the cartographer, as the coarse line of the woodcut could not. A woodcut surface has only two tones, black or white; but the dots or flicks of the engraver's tool could produce the delicate effects of shading or stipple required for relief or water features. The fine point of the graver, moving freely across the copper, was far better adapted than the meticulous woodcut technique to the lettering of place-names, which must be legible yet condensed, appropriately related by its size to the importance of the features represented, and harmonious with the rest of the design. This quality gave the copper-plate engraver a further advantage in rendering the subtle and profuse detail of Renaissance ornament. He could work much faster than the engraver on wood, whose smaller output placed him at a commercial disadvantage not compensated by his simpler printing process.

A wood-block and a copper plate had perhaps about the same expectation of life; although the wood-block suffered less wear in printing, it was less easily reworked or repaired. It is estimated that 2,000 to 3,000 impressions might be taken from a plate or block without serious wear; yet by careful husbandry and (if necessary) by retouching of the incised lines, the life of a copper plate could be, and often was, prolonged to a phenomenal span. Thus Saxton's large map of England and Wales, first printed in 1583, was reprinted in the middle of the 18th century and still advertised in a printseller's catalogue as late as 1795.[1] Finally, line-engraved work can be readily deleted, altered or corrected by rubbing or scraping down the lines on the face of the plate and beating up the corresponding part of the back. The long life of copper plates, which these factors made possible, tempted commercially minded map-publishers (as will be seen) to 'pull' and sell impressions long after their geographical content had fallen behind contemporary knowledge. In this respect copper-plate engraving has had a conservative effect in the history of geography.

In spite of the technical accomplishment seen in the three Ptolemaic atlases of the 15th century engraved on copper, the woodcut remained the chosen vehicle for map-reproduction until the middle of the next century, when cartographers of the Netherlands, familiar with metal-working in the construction of mathematical instruments, and printsellers of Italy, supplying a European market for sheet maps, turned again to line-engraving. For maps in books, however, wood-engraving continued in common use until well into the 17th century, although often by printing from old blocks. In over thirty editions of Sebastian Münster's *Cosmographia*, published at Basle from 1550 to 1628, some of the original woodcuts (with many additions) were used throughout for maps and other illustrations.[2] This work may serve as a specimen of a curious device by which German wood-engravers attempted to simplify and shorten their labour. The names and other legends on Münster's maps are printed from metal type, or rather from stereotype plates cast from lines of type and inserted in recesses cut in the wood-block.[3] This technique had the obvious commercial advantage of saving the engraver's time and costs, but it was applied crudely and with little appreciation of its possibilities.

Etching, although the most fluent and 'freehand' of the intaglio processes and so apparently the fittest for map-reproduction, has rarely been applied to the engraving of

---

[1] By Bowles & Carver. We do not know whether this was old stock or new 'pulls' from the old plates. The latest surviving impression of the map has the imprint of John Bowles & Son and may be dated about 1753–64.

[2] See below, pp. 39–40. If we allow the modest figure of 500 copies to an edition, this gives the extraordinary total of over 15,000 impressions from the original blocks, not counting impressions taken from them for use in other books.

[3] Plates 5–7, 10 illustrate this process. See also W. Horn in *Imago Mundi*, VII (1951), pp. 70–73; and below, p. 14.

maps, and as a rule only for making copies or for adding detail to line-engravings. The formal elements in a map were doubtless thought to be better served by line-engraving. A notable etched map is the copy of Saxton's large map made by Wenceslaus Hollar in 1644 for the use of the armies in the Civil Wars and commonly known as the 'Quartermaster's Map'. Hollar is in fact the leading master who has applied this technique to maps. Etched lines may be distinguished by their blunt or square ends from those of a line-engraving, which generally taper to a point.

The publication of maps from copper plates and of text from movable type within one volume became customary from 1570, when the first edition of Ortelius's atlas appeared. This set the printer an awkward problem, particularly when the text was long. Types, which were scarce and costly in the 16th and 17th centuries, had to be distributed immediately after printing, for use in setting the next book; and, to avoid the heavy expense of resetting his text, the printer who anticipated a demand for reissues of his atlas tended to print off a large number of sheets for future sale. The copper plates on which the maps were engraved called for different treatment; if their life was to be prolonged to give a satisfactory return on the capital investment which they represented, they had to be subjected to the wear and tear of the printing process no more than was necessary. The 17th-century printer of atlases reconciled these conflicting claims by running off an edition of the text pages large enough to provide for a number of reissues, leaving the map pages blank; as a reissue was called for, only as many impressions were taken from the copper plates as would satisfy the immediate demand. The plates might be altered between issues, and so, in the atlases of Speed, Jansson, and Blaeu, successive issues are found with the same setting of text but different states of the maps. Alterations in the plates are sometimes the only evidence for dating an edition of an atlas, when the text is unchanged and (as often) the title-page date uncorrected.

Printed maps were coloured by hand until the 19th century.[1] Whether a fine line-engraving is improved by colour is a matter of taste; Ortelius, who began his career as an illuminator of maps, expressed his preference for uncoloured impressions of maps.[2] In the 16th and 17th centuries the colouring, or 'illumination', of maps was a specialised skill following well-defined conventions, which will be discussed later.

The terms used in carto-bibliography, or the description of engraved sheet maps, differ from those of book-bibliography. A single example of a map printed (or 'pulled') from a block or plate is an *impression*; if taken before engraving is completed, it is a *proof*. Impressions showing differences in the block or plate (i.e. alterations, additions or deletions) are in different *states*, or from different states of the block or plate. An *issue* consists of all impressions pulled from a block or plate at one time; a *reissue* is a fresh batch of impressions from the block or plate in the same state. An *edition* consists of impressions from a distinct state of the block or plate.[3]

Latin phrases found in the signatures or legends of engraved maps may be roughly classified as follows:

(*a*) When referring to the cartographer or draughtsman: *delineavit, descripsit, invenit, auctore.*

(*b*) When referring to the engraver: *sculpsit (sculp., sc.), fecit, caelavit, incidit (incidente).*

(*c*) When referring to the printer or publisher: *excudit (excud., exc.), formis, sumptibus, apud, ex officina.*

---

[1] But see p. 14 below. Hand-colouring was used by the Ordnance Survey as late as 1902.
[2] In a letter to his nephew Ortelianus, 4 January 1595.
[3] There is no general agreement on the use of the terms 'issue' and 'edition' when applied to maps. The practice here described is that of the British Museum Catalogue of Printed Maps.

Finally, it must be remembered that a plate bearing the signature of an engraver may not be wholly from his hand. It is probable that in a workshop, of the type to be described later, different craftsmen were employed in engraving the various component parts of a map. As a rule, no doubt, the master whose signature is on the plate cut the face of the map, sometimes also perhaps the place names and the more spectacular ornament; but it is clear, from the evidence of unfinished proofs,[1] that he left to his journeymen, trained in his style, the commonplace tasks of adding mechanical detail (e.g. the shading of sea and hills), stereotyped ornament (as in borders), and repetitive legends such as imprints or compass directions.

III. THE MAP TRADE

The reproduction of maps by the printing press brought them within the reach of a new public. It introduced the ordinary man to precise geographical ideas of location, extent, and direction of which he had been only dimly aware before. This was an intellectual revolution effected by a technical and commercial innovation; and the business of printing and publishing maps has since the 15th century more powerfully controlled the diffusion of geographical knowledge than even the written or printed word. We need to understand how this trade grew and was organised.

Booksellers controlled most of the commerce in printed maps in the 15th century. The first printed map (a world diagram, or mappamundi, in St Isidore's *Etymologiae*, Augsburg, 1472) was a book-illustration, as were most maps printed before 1500. It was a German book-printer, Conrad Sweynheym, who taught their craft to the Italian engravers of Ptolemy's maps for the Rome edition of 1478 (and perhaps also to the engravers of the Bologna edition of 1477). The early printer sold his books in his shop, and there was at first no separate trade in engraved maps. In Mediterranean cities a brisk production of manuscript coastal charts and decorative maps continued to supply the needs of seamen and collectors. By the end of the 15th century printed sheet maps had also become popular, and the specialised map- and print-seller had made his appearance. He too controlled all the stages of production and publication: he and his assistants drew the maps, engraved, printed and coloured them, sold them over the counter of his shop and perhaps exported them. Such a craftsman and merchant was Francesco Rosselli, who set up in business in Florence soon after 1489. The inventory of his shop made in 1527[2] lists in detail his stock of 'forme', or blocks and plates on which his maps were engraved, and of printed sheet maps.[3] Rosselli sold his own maps but probably not those of other cartographers. The printer was still his own retail mapseller, and the publisher, as a middleman between the printing and retail trades, was superfluous.

By the middle of the 16th century a more elaborate trade organisation was required to supply the European map market, which was dominated by the work of Italian engravers. The principal centres of map production and dealing were Venice, where the houses of F. Bertelli, G. F. Camocio and Paolo Forlani were established, and Rome, where Antonio Salamanca, Antonio Lafreri and C. Duchetti worked. These men may be properly called publishers, for they sold their maps not only in their own shops but also to other engravers or dealers for re-sale. The employees of the Italian printseller, himself often an engraver, were engaged in engraving new maps, making copies of other men's maps, or re-working and altering plates acquired from other dealers. The extent of the stock thus formed by a

---

[1] Such as those of the maps engraved by Hondius for Speed's *Theatre of the Empire of Great Britaine*, 1611–12.
[2] See R. Almagià in *Imago Mundi*, VIII (1952).
[3] The best known of these is G. M. Contarini's world map (1506), engraved by Rosselli. Of this, the first printed map to show the New World, the only known copy was acquired by the British Museum in 1923.

leading merchant can be estimated from the catalogue of his prints and maps published by Lafreri about 1573;[1] this lists over 500 pieces, about a quarter of which were maps and plans. But Lafreri (like other publishers) retailed the output not only of his own engravers but also of the other Roman and Venetian workshops. The Italian mapsellers may be credited with the idea of a comprehensive collection of modern maps, or world atlas;[2] and in a 'Lafreri atlas', assembled for a customer, the publisher's own stock is commonly supplemented by impressions purchased from other printshops, e.g. those of Camocio or Forlani. Similarly, in collections formed by a Venetian dealer such as Bertelli, some of the maps bear the imprint of his trade rivals.

The maps of the Venetian (and, less commonly, the Roman) workshops were fed to the European market through the great book fairs ('*Messen*') held twice a year[3] at Frankfort-on-Main, Cologne and Leipzig. As clearing houses for the international trade in books and prints, the fairs were frequented by sellers and buyers from the countries of southern, central and western Europe. The official catalogue of the Frankfort fair of 1573,[4] published by the dealer G. Willer, gives an interesting list of the maps and atlases exposed for sale. Here we find the early editions of Ortelius's atlas (1570–1573), 14 maps by cartographers of Germany and the Low Countries, and no less than 68 sheet maps from Italian shops, all but a few of which were Venetian.

The cartographic industry of the Netherlands and Rhineland, which in the last three decades of the 16th century supplanted that of Italy, was more solidly founded on scientific method and systematic presentation. Abraham Ortelius's *Theatrum orbis terrarum* of 1570 was no haphazard set of maps like the Italian atlases, but a methodically planned collection of the best maps available, engraved in a uniform size by his own artists. Perhaps the strength of the craft-guilds in north-western Europe explains the fact that the map-publishing houses of this period and throughout the 17th century were essentially groups of working engravers; the workshops of Mercator at Duisburg, of Frans Hogenberg and of Theodore de Bry at Cologne, of the de Jode and van Langeren families at Antwerp, of Hondius, Jansson, Blaeu and others at Amsterdam were primarily occupied in the drawing and engraving of maps. Yet, in a period of expanding demand and increasing competition, the development of more elaborate commercial relations in the map-trade became inevitable.

A detailed and vivid picture of this trade can be drawn from two priceless collections of contemporary documents: the business records of the great Antwerp printer Christophe Plantin (1514–89)[5] in the Musée Plantin-Moretus, Antwerp, and the correspondence of Ortelius for the years 1556–98, preserved by the Dutch Church in London.[6] Plantin, who started printing in 1555, published few maps, although fourteen editions of Ortelius's *Theatrum* (from 1579) and Waghenaer's *Spieghel der zeevaert* (1584) and *Thresoor der zeevaert* (1592), the first printed sea-atlases, came from his press. As a middleman, however, selling maps, globes, and geographical instruments produced by other firms or workshops, Plantin carried on an immense business. The names of all the leading cartographers of the Netherlands appear in the catalogue of maps sold by him between 1555 and 1593 or in his account-books, as in debt to him for materials and services, or in credit for maps supplied. Annually from 1558 Plantin visited the Frankfort fair to replenish his stocks;[7] and he has left a colour-

[1] Reprinted by F. Ehrle, *Roma prima di Sisto V* (1908), pp. 53–59.

[2] See Chapter III, p. 43 below.　　　　　　　　　[3] At Quadragesima and Michaelmas.

[4] Reprinted by L. Bagrow in *Imago Mundi*, V (1948), pp. 53–62.

[5] The extracts relating to cartographers are printed and discussed by J. Denucé, *Oud-Nederlandsche kaart-makers in betrekking met Plantijn* (1912).

[6] Printed by J. H. Hessels, *Abrahami Ortelii . . . epistulae* (1887). The originals were sold by auction in London in 1955.

[7] It was at the Frankfort fair that Ortelius first met Mercator, in 1554, and Plantin, in 1558.

ful account of his hazardous journey in 1585, during the siege of Antwerp, when he travelled from Amsterdam to Hamburg by sea, thence to Frankfort by coach, and on to the Cologne fair in the company of Ortelius. Through his agents abroad Plantin exported maps to his customers in foreign countries, including England; and his records are our main source of information on the diffusion of 16th-century maps and globes. From them we learn also of contemporary trade practices, such as the agreement by which Filips Galle obtained from Hogenberg exclusive rights to sell the *Civitates orbis terrarum*[1] in Antwerp.

Ortelius, as a compiler and publisher of geographical works, also purchased maps extensively but for a different purpose. Like all book- and map-sellers of his day, he sold works printed at his own expense direct to customers, but he does not seem to have dealt much in the publications of other firms after the appearance of his atlas. His agents in foreign cities were instructed to procure or to copy 'the best descriptions of each region', and these served as material from which his own engravers copied.

At the end of the 16th century the centre of the cartographic industry shifted from the southern to the northern Netherlands, from Antwerp to Amsterdam; and during the next century the integration of the processes of production and distribution became closer than ever. Stocks of engraved copper plates; equipment for typecasting, engraving, printing, colouring and binding; and craftsmen skilled in all these trades were concentrated in the family house of a master such as Hondius, Jansson, Blaeu, Visscher, Danckerts, or de Wit;[2] and these men sold their output both wholesale and retail, i.e. to other mapsellers or direct to their own customers. The industry was, so to speak, organised 'vertically'; it was also highly capitalised, and we may contrast Lafreri's modest stock of about 500 items in 1573 with the 1,500 or more plates that must have been owned by the firm of Blaeu or that of de Wit a century later.[3] Trade relations between the rival houses were close,[4] and partnerships were formed in this period for the publication of atlases or maps, as for that of books; thus variant copies of the *Atlas Minor* of Jodocus Hondius (1607) bear on their title-pages the names of three independent publishers. Nevertheless, competition, controlled by no copyright law, was keen and not always scrupulous.[5] The prize was an international market, for throughout the 17th century Dutch maps were exported in immense numbers.[6]

In other countries the organisation of the map-trade developed more slowly. French production, mainly controlled by natives of the Low Countries or Northern France, did not rival the Dutch until the second half of the 17th century, and the German industry, also in close contact with that of the Netherlands, later still; and at the end of the century there was a revival of activity in Venice, associated with the famous name of V. M. Coronelli.

In England the bookselling industry was highly organised in the 16th century and controlled the printing and distribution of woodcuts, whether as broadsides or as book-illustrations; but no machinery for the separate marketing of maps and prints existed before about 1600. The maps of European firms were despatched to their English customers (some of whom are named in Plantin's ledgers) either direct or through an agent in London; and English craftsmen were slow to learn the technique of copper-plate engraving from the

[1] See Chapter IV, p. 47.

[2] The organisation of such a house is described in Chapter VI, p. 59.

[3] Pieter van der Aa's vast compilation, *La Galerie agréable du monde* (1729), contained impressions from over 3,000 plates, mainly of the previous century.

[4] The atlas of W. J. Blaeu, for instance, was developed from a stock of plates which he acquired in 1629 from his rival in trade H. Hondius; and the 11-volume edition of Jansson's atlas published in 1658 was completed by Blaeu's atlas of China (1665).

[5] See Chapter VI, pp. 59–60.

[6] And, at the end of the century, Dutch engraved plates also. See pp. 8, 71.

Flemish masters. The earliest map known to have been engraved on copper by an Englishman is that of the Holy Land (Pl. 31) published in the Bishops' Bible of 1572; its engraver Humphry Cole, goldsmith at the Mint and the leading English instrument-maker of his day, proudly declares his map 'Graven bi Humfray Cole goldsmith a English man born in yᵉ North'. Yet only eight of the 35 maps in Saxton's atlas (engraved 1574–79) are signed by English engravers; and those of Speed's *Theatre of the Empire of Great Britaine* (published in 1611–12) were sent to Amsterdam to be engraved in the workshop of Jodocus Hondius. For want of publishers, the English cartographer depended on patrons for the printing of his maps in the 16th century. Saxton's county maps were commissioned and financed by a private patron, with state support, and we do not know through what channels his maps were sold; Norden's *Speculum Britanniae* failed because he found no patron.[1]

By the end of the century several English engravers were at work[2] and the first London printsellers, John Sudbury and George Humble, had opened their shop.[3] At their expense the engraving of Speed's maps was begun by Hondius about 1605, and the *Theatre* which appeared in 1611–12 over their imprint was the first large-scale enterprise in commercial map-publication in Britain. Its success was immediate, and reprints of Speed's maps satisfied the English market until a fresh demand was created by the Civil Wars. This was met partly by importing the new English maps of Blaeu and Jansson (copied from those of Speed), partly by reprints from the old plates of Saxton, Norden, Symonson and others which had come into the possession of printer-sellers like Thomas Jenner, Peter Stent and his successor John Overton. Few new maps were drawn or engraved (perhaps for want of capital) until the revival of English cartography at the Restoration.[4] Even then the London map-trade, in spite of its greatly expanded production, remained largely dependent on the Dutch industry. From Holland were imported printing types and the fine paper needed for map printing; from Holland also, technical ideas such as Blaeu's improved printing press and the recipe for the best ink for copper-plate printing.[5] Above all the capital needed for the survey and engraving of new maps was scarce, and patrons and subscribers were unreliable.[6] The mapseller, as a businessman, found it cheaper to reprint from his stock of old plates and to import Dutch or French maps and even plates, which he retouched and supplied with his own imprint. Pepys tells us that for his sea-atlases John Seller 'had bought the old worn Dutch copper plates for old copper and had refreshed them in many places'; and it was of Seller's *English Pilot* that a (perhaps ironical) panegyrist wrote:

> 'This of your Book, and you, I may foretell,
> What SELLER made, be sure will SELL.'

The English trade could not dispense with imports from Holland and France until the 18th century, when (in 1712) a duty of 30 per cent was for the first time levied on imported prints and maps.

[1] See Chapter V, pp. 51–53.
[2] Stimulated no doubt by the example of Hondius and other Flemish or Dutch engravers exiled in London from 1583 to about 1593.
[3] In Pope's head Alley, near the Royal Exchange. The first map with Sudbury's imprint dates from 1599.
[4] See Chapter VIII.
[5] Both described by Joseph Moxon, *Mechanick Exercises* (1683), vol. ii.
[6] When John Ogilby's subscribers failed him, he was forced to pay for his surveys by organising a standing lottery in 1673; and 'the first scheme for a triangulation of England', that of John Adams, found no support. See E. G. R. Taylor's article (*Geographical Journal*, vol. xc, 1937, pp. 529–540) on contemporary cartographical projects; this quotes an estimate for a set of new county maps (probably planned by John Seller) which amounted to £1,441 5s., including a shilling a mile for the simplified survey, £1 5s. for each copper plate, and £8 a plate for engraving.

During the 17th century the productive and distributive sides of the English book industry tended to become more specialised.[1] This was not practicable in the map- and print-trade, in which the operations of engraving, printing, and sale were carried on under the same roof, and (in addition) the mapseller and his assistants might be professional surveyors and instrument-makers.[2] This alliance of technical and commercial activities called for more substantial capital resources than were usually needed in the book-trade and, as on the Continent, it had two consequences: the concentration of stocks and of business in the hands of a comparatively small number of houses, and the development of partnerships or joint-stock enterprises in publication. The names of the large mapsellers in the half-century after 1670 – Seller, Morden, Lea, Berry, Overton, Thornton – are repeatedly found in combination on their maps. The practice became even commoner in the later 18th century, and multiple imprints (e.g. those of Bowen, Kitchin, Bowles, Sayer, Rocque, Jefferys) or, *tout court*, that of 'the Mapsellers of London', occur repeatedly. The maps of *The Large English Atlas*, published from 1749, bear the imprints of no fewer than four mapsellers.

That popular geographical ideas generally lagged far behind the knowledge of contemporary geographers is due in no small measure to the 'conservatising' effect of the commercial conditions in which the European map-trade worked. The 17th-century successors of the 'scholar-cartographers' Mercator and Blaeu were for the most part tradesmen interested in keeping costs down and sales up. As a geographer[3] complained, they constantly copied from one another, 'introducing more and more errors and yet putting on their maps: Tabula nova, novissima, exactissima, recens curata, etc.'; and he adds that they are almost all alike, 'so that whoever has the maps of one has in fact those of the others'.[4] New ideas, such as John Adams's ill-fated plan for a geodetic survey of England, were of course unprofitable. In cartography, it has been said, plagiarism is commoner and more easily disguised than in any other activity except music. Only limited copyright protection was secured to the mapseller of the 16th and 17th centuries[5] by the grant of a privilege, usually for not more than ten years; and to copy a map was cheaper than to make a survey or to compile a map from up-to-date information. Not until 1734 did an English statute offer legal protection to the owner of copyright in an engraved map or chart.

In the 18th century the gap between popular and scientific geography was somewhat narrowed. New surveys were made and new maps drawn by cartographers who were also accomplished astronomers, like the Cassini family in France, or scholars, like d'Anville, or land surveyors, like Rocque and Jefferys in England and Samuel Holland in America, or marine hydrographers, like J. N. Bellin, Captain Cook and Murdoch Mackenzie. Commercial mapsellers in all countries continued to draw profits from their old plates. The county maps of Saxton and Speed were reprinted for the last time about 1770,[6] and the charts of Seller and Thornton (for the misguidance of mariners!) until the end of the century. But the trade was now largely controlled by men who were not merely shopkeepers but also map-makers; and patrons had become more discriminating.

[1] In 1700 London had 42 printers, 188 booksellers, and only 25 men who practised both trades. (M. Plant, *The English Booktrade*, 1939, p. 64.)

[2] Joseph Moxon was both a master printer and a chart-maker – an unusual combination.

[3] E. D. Hauber, *Versuch einer umständlichen Historie der Land-Charten*, 1724.

[4] This may be compared with Richard Gough's remark (in 1780) that 'since maps have been published, the several sorts . . . are supposed to amount at least to 16,000: but of these not above 1,700 are originals'. This estimate was derived from that made by a German geographer in 1747; see below, p. 62.

[5] Sometimes to the cartographer, e.g. to Saxton in 1577 and to Norden in 1592.

[6] See also p. 3, note 1.

Above all, Governments had realised, as seldom before, the necessity for reliable maps. Official surveys, such as those of North America during the French and Revolutionary Wars, were no longer suffered to remain in manuscript, but were published either by a department of State (as when the Admiralty printed Des Barres' *Atlantic Neptune* in 1777) or, more commonly, by a commercial mapseller. The title Geographer to the King (or to other royal persons), which originated in France and Spain in the 16th century, came into use in England at the Restoration;[1] but in this country until the middle of the 18th century the style was little more than an adjunct to trade (like 'by appointment to the Queen' to-day). When Thomas Jefferys held it, however, the office was in fact that of official map-publisher; and it was no accident that the first Ordnance Survey map to be printed – that of Kent – was in 1801 published by Jefferys' successor in business, William Faden. The business records of the same firm, now in an American library,[2] illustrate the scale and complexity of the international map-trade in the 18th century. In all parts of Europe Jefferys and Faden had correspondents who offered maps for sale or ordered English maps and instruments.

IV. THE HISTORY OF CONVENTIONAL SIGNS

A map is a topographical drawing, and topography may be called the portraiture of places. To display the features of his subject in their true relation to one another, that is, proportionally correct in extent and in distance apart, the map-maker must observe a uniform horizontal scale throughout his drawing. This is only possible if the area represented is visualised from a point vertically above it; the smaller the scale the more remote is the map-maker's viewpoint. Here is a dilemma which has perplexed every cartographer who has attempted to draw accurate maps. For the landscape which is his subject is not flat like his paper. It is made up of all kinds of features which, seen from the ground, stand up in relief and stretch out in perspective: hills and valleys, trees, houses and other buildings. A map is not – it cannot afford to be – merely a geometrical diagram in which the horizontal distances and relationships are correct; it must somehow suggest the appearance of its subject as it is seen by the observer on the ground. Conventional signs, or symbols, are the device by which these two viewpoints are reconciled and the conflicting demands of accuracy and visual effect satisfied. 'Chorographie', wrote William Cuningham in 1559 of the mapping of small areas, 'consisteth rather in describing the qualitie and figure, then the bignes and quantitie of any thinge'; and by this he meant much the same as the modern writer who has remarked that 'a good symbol is one that can be recognized without a legend'.[3]

Recognition of a symbol implies its immediate identification with the object which we see in elevation from the ground. The ideal symbol is obviously a picture which reproduces our visual image; and pictorial symbols have always been, and still are, used by cartographers. But while pictures of a mountain or town or group of trees, seen in elevation or profile, reveal the vertical character of the subject, they conceal its length and breadth, that is, its plan. To meet this difficulty, map-makers of the 16th and 17th centuries raised their viewpoint and drew such subjects in perspective or bird's-eye view[4] and later in plan, and

---

[1] A list of the French 'géographes du roi', 1560–1865, is given by J. van der Maelen in *Bulletin de la Société Géographique d'Anvers*, vol. i (1877), pp. 477–484. John Ogilby enjoyed the title of Cosmographer to the King (Charles II); both Seller and Joseph Moxon that of Hydrographer to the King. In the 18th century Emanuel Bowen was appointed geographer to both George II and Louis XV.

[2] The William L. Clements Library in the University of Michigan. Extracts have been printed by G. Kish in *Imago Mundi*, IV (1947), pp. 75–77.

[3] E. Raisz, *General Cartography* (1938), p. 118.

[4] As in the famous atlas of town plans by Braun and Hogenberg (see Chap. IV). But maps of much larger areas were sometimes drawn in bird's-eye view, e.g. G. Boileau's Savoy (1556) and the curious maps of English counties by George Bickham (1754). The larger the subject, of course, the greater the distortion of scale in different parts of such a map.

the conventional signs on smaller-scale maps followed suit. The history of the symbols used by map-makers shows a gradual trend towards the vertical viewpoint and the substitution of geometrical for pictorial signs; and their maps have lost in decorative effect what they have gained in accuracy.

Among the conventions borrowed from manuscript maps by the earliest map-engravers were a few geometrical signs, such as the circle with a dot or a cross in its centre for towns; but most of the symbols were pictorial. Hills were generally represented by slabs of rock or conical 'sugarloaf' peaks shaded at the edges; mountain ranges by rope-like and similar designs; forests by groups of trees;[1] the sea by undulating lines, and its coasts by hatching on the seaward side; rivers by double banks, usually with flowing form-lines following the direction of the stream, and their sources often by little ponds; cities and towns by clusters of buildings of appropriate character, with walls, towers and house-roofs; roads (where shown) at first by a single dotted, later by a double, line. These conventions of design, or variations on them, supplemented by those of colour, remained in use until the 18th century, and some of them later still. The practice of engravers in wood and on metal differed little, although for the clumsier woodcut technique simpler forms were usually adopted; but German regional cartographers of the 16th century, notably Philipp Apian (Pl. 10b), introduced a series of ingenious and graphic pictorial symbols.

With the maturity of copper-plate engraving in the 16th century, the old symbols were refined and elaborated, usually for decorative rather than geographical reasons, and new ones were introduced. A greater variety appeared in the form of mountains, which were now generally (though not uniformly) shaded on the east, perhaps because, as has been ingeniously suggested,[2] 'sensible draughtsmen have always worked with the light on their left'. The conical sugarloaf was still common, as in Saxton's maps. There was little change in the representation of woods, but several new fashions appeared in that of water features. Stippling, or a dotted surface, was a simple technical process for the copper-plate engraver, and this was very commonly used for the sea (Pl. 13, 16), but we also find many varieties of wave forms, sometimes differentiated from the calmer enclosed waters of gulfs or lakes which were indicated by distinctive shading or by stippling (Pl. 18, 25). Towards the end of the century Flemish engravers, simplifying the wave forms, created an elegant 'shot-silk' effect by zig-zag shading (Pl. 37, 44).[3] Occasionally the sea was left blank. Coasts were still shaded outwards; but on the printed charts which made their appearance at the end of the century the coastline was commonly drawn in elevation, reefs or sands were stippled, rivers appeared as wide estuaries, and soundings and anchorages were marked in the form used to-day.

For towns, pictorial symbols remained popular. These were drawn in perspective or elevation and were adapted to the character of the town, showing (for instance) whether it was fortified or not, and to its size, which was indicated by the number of houses shown beside the church spire; a circle with a dot in the middle was generally drawn at the church door to mark the town centre.[4] For hamlets and country houses the circle alone was used. The various town symbols were explained in tables of conventional signs, which seem to have originated in Germany (Pl. 10b) and to have been introduced in England at the end of the century by William Smith, herald and topographer, after his residence in Nuremberg; John

---

[1] The distinction in the drawing of deciduous and coniferous woods goes back to the 15th century (Pl. 1).
[2] By E. Lynam. The convention has held its own to this day.
[3] An early form of this convention, on a woodcut map, is seen in Pl. 3a.
[4] The circle alone was generally used for towns in woodcut maps, for simplicity of engraving, and in road maps where distances had to be measured precisely.

Norden, no doubt taking the idea from Smith, was the first English cartographer to add them to printed maps, and this helped to standardise conventions. A comparison of the table in a German map (Lusatia, by B. Scultetus, 1593) with that in Norden's Sussex (1595) illustrates the different social conditions in the two countries: the German map has symbols for cities, walled towns and open towns, castles or country houses of two kinds, monasteries, villages with and without churches, and mountains; Norden's list (Pl. 36) has market towns, parishes, hamlets, noblemen's houses, 'howses of gent. &c', castles, 'religious places', chapels and beacons.[1]

In Norden's, as in Saxton's, maps the numerous parks, indicated by a ring-fence surrounding a few trees, point to the growth of enclosure under the Tudors. The signs in Norden's table are generally geometrical, but his and Speed's maps and town plans are sprinkled with many delightful pictorial symbols for structures important in the social and economic life of the people: crosses, beacons, gallows, wind- and water-mills, drying frames for fishing nets, limekilns, pounds and pinfolds, cockpits, shambles, maypoles and stocks. Norden's roads, the first to appear in English printed maps, are shown by double dotted lines,[2] bridges (as in Saxton's maps) by double lines like a tiny arch; Speed, in his town-plans, distinguishes bridges of timber and of stone. Battle symbols, already found in manuscript maps, appear in Norden's, Speed's and other maps printed about 1600, as clashing ranks of armed men or as tents;[3] and a few major antiquities, as the Roman or 'Pictes' wall, were represented by simple pictorial images.

The Dutch engraver-publishers of the 17th century and their imitators made few changes in map conventions, although they varied and elaborated their design (often fancifully) and heightened relief by deeper shading. How little symbols changed may be judged from John Ogilby's list in 1675:[4] 'The *Road* . . . is express'd by double Black Lines if included by Hedges, or Prick'd Lines if open . . . *Capital Towns* are describ'd Ichnographically [i.e. in plan] . . . but the *Lesser Towns* and *Villages*, with the *Mansion Houses, Castles, Churches, Mills, Beacons, Woods,* &c. Scenographically, or in Prospect. *Bridges* are usually noted with a Circular Line like an Arch . . . *Rivers* are *Decypher'd* by a treble wav'd Line or more, and the lesser *Rills* or *Brooks* by a single or double Line, according to their Eminency.' Ogilby here discloses two improvements made in his century: the drawing of large towns in plan instead of perspective (a Dutch innovation associated especially with the representation of fortified places), and the greater variety of symbols employed and more discriminating use of them (e.g. the distinction between fenced and unfenced roads). New signs indeed proliferated, especially for towns, which in Ogilby's map of Kent are classified in ten types, each with its separate symbol. A few other 17th-century innovations may be noted. Coast lines were sometimes shaded on the landward side (Pl. 65), and the sea was more usually unshaded. The practice of drawing relief features as if seen from above, with 'vertical' shading on each slope, was introduced; this was an important new convention, which defined the plan of a hill or range (although giving no precise idea of its height), and could distinguish steeper slopes by greater density of shading.

In England, as in no other country, the 18th century was a period of experiment and expansion in agriculture, of industrial achievement and commercial prosperity, of great

---

[1] The table in Norden's Middlesex (1593) adds 'caracters' for royal palaces, bishops' sees, sites of battles, 'decayde places', hunting lodges, and mills.

[2] German road maps, from before 1500, had used a single dotted line (Pl. 3b).

[3] Norden also (in his map of Middlesex, 1593) used a Greek cross to indicate a battle-site. From the clashing soldiers, already found some 30 years earlier in German printed maps, is derived the modern symbol of crossed swords for a battle-site.

[4] In the preface to his road-atlas, *Britannia Vol. I.*

landed estates, of development of the roads and navigable waterways, of political growth, of technical achievement and historical curiosity. Many of these social changes are reflected in map conventions, which continued to multiply and to become more realistic. The English technique of representation owed much to that of France, where the great Cassini map employed a phenomenal number of distinctive symbols;[1] but native cartographers invented a host of new signs illustrating diverse aspects of human activity, while the representation of natural features remained generally conservative. Coal and lead mines, post mills and smock mills, turnpikes and post roads, medicinal waters, schools and religious benefices, antiquities – for all these, and much else, we find neatly drawn separate symbols, which were not superseded by simpler and more geometrical forms until the end of the century. The most striking innovations were in the representation of antiquities, communications, and land surface. The table on Isaac Taylor's map of Hampshire (1759) gives symbols for 'old [religious] foundations, castles demolish'd, bishops' palaces demolish'd, barrows & tumuli'; each class has more than one different sign, and barrows no fewer than four. The same cartographer used a neat symbol to indicate the limit of navigation in a river; and mileages on post roads were inserted in many maps. The English map-maker, generally also a professional estate surveyor, flattered his patrons among the landed gentry not only by setting their coats of arms in the margins, but also by drawing their houses, parks and plantations in detail on his map. Finally, John Rocque, a surveyor of Huguenot origin, used a great variety of symbols, borrowed from contemporary French cartographers or from the technique of estate survey, to depict in ambitious detail different types of land surfaces and utilisation (Pl. 82). His county maps show us where the limits of cultivation and waste lay, whether a field was meadow, pasture, or under crops (corn, hops, etc.), how private gardens and plantations were laid out, and much other significant detail.

Rocque's preference of the plan (or 'vertical' viewpoint) is apparent also in his consistent use of vertical shading for hills, which were still drawn in perspective or as 'hairy caterpillars' by most of his contemporaries; but contours, the most exact device for describing changes in height, had in Rocque's day already been introduced, although they were not adopted by map-makers until many years later. While spot heights did not generally appear on printed land maps until the time of the Ordnance Survey, soundings had been marked on engraved sea-charts since the 16th century; and the submarine contour, introduced by a Dutch hydrographer[2] in 1729, was developed simply by drawing a line through points of equal depth. By the end of the century French military cartographers had extended the practice to land maps. The 18th century saw great advances in the techniques of marine survey and of chart-making, although conventions of drawing changed little; but we may note, as an innovation, that form-lines, drawn parallel to the shore and suggesting contours, had generally superseded the old coastal hatching (Pl. 77).

V. LETTERING, DECORATION, AND COLOUR

Lettering

The map-maker's art is graphic and linear; he expresses geographical facts by drawn outlines and symbols. Conventional signs are a device which enables a feature to be recognised without the necessity of providing a written label such as 'mountain', 'wood' or 'town'. Yet legends cannot be dispensed with, although the skilful and conscientious cartographer will aim at Mercator's reputation of 'banishing them from the map'. In all but outline maps,

---

[1] Including, for instance, four different types of gallows.

[2] N. S. Cruquius; followed by P. Buache, 1737. Their use of the device was preceded, and may have been suggested, by Halley's 'isogonic' lines in his chart of magnetic variation, 1700.

lettering must be used for the title, for information about the scale, compass points and other 'memorables', and for place-names. All these legends, especially the names which are written over the face of the map, have to be harmoniously combined with the geographical outlines and decoration; they must be easily read but economical of space; and the character and importance of features must be indicated by grading, in size and form, the lettering selected for place-names. To these problems, which still arouse controversy to-day, cartographers of different periods have found solutions satisfying the conditions of their engraving technique and reflecting contemporary fashions in handwriting and lettering. That this is a vital element in map design is shown by the intimate alliance which existed for over two centuries between the arts of calligraphy and cartography.

The wood-engraver, painfully carving his letters in relief, used a technique akin to that of cutting punches for type-casting; his alphabets were on the whole more formal, and it is not surprising to find even letterpress types adopted on woodcut maps. Engraving on copper is, however, a freehand operation, and from the middle of the 16th century letter-forms on line-engraved maps were derived from those of contemporary cursive handwriting, which, as cartographers from Mercator onward recognised, had the combined formality and freedom necessary in map legends.

Before Mercator's time map-engravers experimented with a variety of inscriptional lettering and book-hands. In the 15th-century Italian editions of Ptolemy,[1] with maps engraved on copper, the legends are entirely done in finely proportioned Roman capitals of different sizes derived from monumental inscriptions (Pl. 1); but the maps of the first German edition (that of Ulm, 1482), like other woodcut maps of the time, use capitals only for the names of continents, countries and oceans, sometimes enclosed in scrolls or boxes. For all other names and legends small letters ('minuscules') were employed; the more angular forms were adapted from gothic, the more rounded from the 'caroline' minuscules used in the book-hands of contemporary scribes and letter-cutters. In Johann Schnitzer's world map of 1482 in the Ulm Ptolemy (Pl. 2) both styles of lettering may be seen, but the distinction between pointed gothic and rounded 'roman' (in both upright and cursive forms) soon became more clearly observed. In the engraving of maps, as in the design of printing types, national tastes asserted themselves, and gothic lettering has since the early 16th century been preferred by German cartographers (Pl. 10b).

The labour-saving practice of printing place-names from stereotype metal plates inserted in the wood-block was introduced in the 15th century and generally adopted by German cartographers during the first half of the 16th.[2] This technique is found in some or all maps of many important woodcut atlases, including the Venice Ptolemy of 1511, the great Strassburg Ptolemy of 1513 and its revision of 1522, the Cosmographies of Peter Apian (1533) and Sebastian Münster (1544), and Münster's edition of Ptolemy (1540). Some copies (e.g. of the 1511 and 1513 Ptolemies) have the names of countries and seas printed in red; this practice, made possible by the use of detachable blocks for the names, is the only instance of colour printing applied to maps before the 19th century. For the most part the types chosen were roman or italic, with gothic and roman capitals for the names of provinces (Pl. 5–7). The mechanical character of the lettering thus produced is easily detected; it does not harmonise with the flexible line of the cartographer, nor could it be fitted with the necessary precision into the blank spaces of the map.

[1] And in Cardinal Nicholas of Cusa's Central Europe, the only line-engraved map produced north of the Alps in the 15th century, if we except the engravings in the Lyons edition (1488) of Breydenbach's *Peregrinationes in Terram Sanctam*.

[2] Examples of the technique may be seen in Plates 5–7, 10. In the 17th century Robert Hooke experimented with the adaptation of movable lettering to maps printed from copper plates.

When copper came back into vogue for the engraving of maps, italic writing, developed by scribes of the Papal chancery from cursive caroline minuscules, had already been adopted by humanists for the writing of Latin and introduced into book-printing by Aldus Manutius at Venice. Although it was a cartographer, Gerard Mercator, who made the flowing italic hand popular in north-west Europe, his copy-book of 1540, 'the oldest specimen of cursive handwriting in the Low Countries',[1] makes no reference to its use in maps but commends it merely as the proper script for Latin texts, 'elegant in form, easy to write, and exceptionally legible'. Italic became popular with map-engravers not only because it was suitable for writing Latin, the *lingua franca* of map legends from the 15th to the 18th centuries; they found too that its qualities, which were readily reproduced on the copper plate, enabled names to be correctly and neatly placed and to be elaborated by flourishes and ligatures which contributed to the decorative effect of the map. Although the vernacular style was retained by German cartographers supplying a national market (Pl. 10b), and gothic has been intermittently used by others for 'display' purposes, italic and roman scripts in combination have held their own in map-lettering to this day.

In maps of different periods the forms of these scripts, following contemporary taste, have varied in the proportion and slope of letters and in the manner of connecting them. Italian engravers of the 16th century (Pl. 11, 12) employed a small and slightly inclined lower-case italic akin to the aldine book-types, with few ligatures, and roman capitals for the more important names. The cartographers of the Netherlands, with Mercator's example before them, preferred a fluent sloping hand with italic capitals which, in larger names, became elaborate arabesques of swash letters and flourished ligatures. Mercator's practice had been sober, but the work of Hogenberg (Pl. 17, 18), van Langeren (Pl. 29), and Hondius (Pl. 37, 38, 39, 43, 46) shows the wanton gaiety with which his successors filled the empty spaces on their maps. By contrast the finely drawn roman capitals which they sometimes used instead of italic (as in Pl. 24, 29) successfully avoid over-emphasis by their lightness and open spacing.

These extravagances, of which Dudley's Italian engraver (Pl. 62, 63) provides an even more striking example, were common in the copy-books of writing-masters. By 1600 the brilliant line of the copper plate had been found to serve the calligrapher's technique no less aptly than the map-maker's, and from this time a close connection existed between the two crafts, especially in England. One of the earliest English copy-books[2] was engraved by Hondius during his residence in London; another[3] by the map-engraver William Hole at the expense of Speed's publishers, John Sudbury and George Humble. The catalogues of the map-publishers Peter Stent and his successor John Overton list manuals by the leading writing-masters of the 17th century, including John Davies and Edward Cocker, and the imprint of Davies's *Writing Schoolemaster* (1667) tells us that it is sold by Overton 'at the Sign of the White Horse in Little Brittain . . . where you may have two famous Maps of the City of London Before and Since the Fire'. John Overton's son and successor Henry published, between 1709 and 1758, a great number of copy-books, in addition to the maps which were his main stock-in-trade; and among other map houses of the 18th century which dealt largely in this business were those of Mount and Page, Robert Sayer, the Bowles family, Thomas Kitchin, and Laurie and Whittle. The engravers employed by these firms turned their hand with equal facility to the reproduction of maps and of scripts. Writing-masters in turn applied themselves to cartography; many manuscript estate maps of the 18th century are signed by such men, and two of the leading masters, George Bickham the elder and

---

[1] J. Denucé, in the introduction to his facsimile edition, *The Treatise of Gerard Mercator* (1930).
[2] *Theatrum Artis Scribendi* (1594). [3] M. Billingsley, *The Pen's Excellencie* (1618).

younger, drew a curious series of English county maps in bird's-eye view.[1]

Yet during the 17th and 18th centuries map-lettering in all countries was modelled as much on the improving design of book types as on that of scripts, although 'display' lettering in great variety continued to appear in titles. In Holland the exuberance of the school of Hondius was less popular than the more sober style of Blaeu, who preferred smaller and more regular lettering and used flourishes and swash letters with restraint (Pl. 55–61). Legends were no longer used for decoration, but were subordinated to the cartographic outlines and to the ornament concentrated round the cartouches and in the border. In the late 17th and early 18th centuries the letter-forms used in maps, like those of type faces in books and 'copper-plate' hands in script, became wider, rounder, and more open; ligatures and swash letters disappeared from the face of the map. Here, as in the parallel development of conventional signs, we see the cartographer bringing the auxiliary elements of his map into subjection to its geographical content.

Although the lettering on 18th-century maps resembles book types, the engraver enjoyed increasing freedom in the appropriate siting and grading of names and legends. Cartographers since the 15th century have followed conservative traditions for the position of place-names in relation to the features which they represent. They have very generally obeyed the convention that all the names on a map should be comfortably legible without turning the map. The two conspicuous exceptions to this rule are river names, which in all maps since the Middle Ages have been written along the course of the stream; and coastal names on charts, which are commonly drawn inland, at right angles to the shore, in such a way that the navigator, following the coast in one direction, must orient his chart correctly to read the names (Pl. 54, 62, 63).

Decoration

That maps should please the eye has been accepted even by scientific cartographers. A map, remarked the French military engineer Bonne about 1800, is so 'dry' an object that opportunities for treating it as a picture must not be lost. Geographical outlines could, of course, not be embroidered,[2] but principles of good design could be applied to the conventional signs, and early maps never lacked 'convenient spare and voide places' to be filled with added ornament and little vignettes or thumbnail sketches. Not only was there the featureless sea, in which sea-monsters and great fish could play and ships ride or sail or do battle; there were also wide unknown land areas where ignorance could be supplied by decorative fancy –

> So geographers, in Afric maps,
> With savage pictures fill their gaps . . .

Finally, the border or frame of the map, in itself a natural subject for ornament, could be expanded to accommodate pictures, heraldic designs, descriptive legends and much else for which there was no room on the face of the map.

The map-maker's opportunities for decorating his work were summed up by William Folkingham, land-surveyor,[3] in his pompous but telling Jacobean way: 'The Tricking of Plots [decoration of maps] consists in Complements, and Compartments. Complements

---

[1] *The British Monarchy* (1754).

[2] Although, from the Middle Ages, maps of countries have been drawn in humorous or symbolic form: Russia as a bear, the Netherlands as a lion (Pl. 41), France as a cock, etc. The outline of Scotland, however, baffled the Italian cartographer Magini, who remarked that it resembled nothing whatever.

[3] *Feudigraphia: the synopsis or epitome of surveying methodized* (1610), pp. 56–58.

comprehende the Flie or Flies [compass indicators], Scale and Compasse [dividers], Kalender, Characters, Colours &c. . . . Compartiments are Blankes or Figures bordered with Anticke Boscage or Crotesko-worke, wherein Evidences[1] or other Memorables may be abreviated. And these may be contrived in Parallelograms, Squares, Circles, Ovalls, Lunaries . . . compassed and tricked ad libitum. Under this Title may also be rainged the Lordes Coate with Crest and Mantells.' Here we see how, in the heyday of map-decoration, cartographers used such formal elements as cartouches and panels, scales, compass-roses, the 'Margent or square stick of Degrees' to elaborate their design and, by the addition of coats of arms of noblemen or cities, to commend their work to patrons and purchasers.

The earliest engraved maps, in striking contrast with contemporary manuscript maps, were, however, austere in their use of decoration. In the 15th century this was usually confined to the borders, drawn in a simple saw-tooth or spiral design;[2] to the faces representing the winds, in which artists exercised their fancy freely (Pl. 2); to conventional signs, particularly town-symbols; and to the scale, where the pair of dividers first appears in German maps of about 1500. There is more variety in the few 15th-century regional maps or town plans, which were enlivened by perspective drawings, by little pictures – e.g. of ships, soldiers, allegorical figures – and by heraldic detail.

The virtuosity of German wood-engravers[3] in the first half of the 16th century developed a profusion of ornament on and round their maps. Formal decoration is not absent; the cartouches usually imitate wood carving, coats of arms abound, the compass indicator and scale are elaborated, legends in florid gothic lettering fill the margins and invade the map. But the design is dominated by a host of intricately drawn naturalistic motives (Pl. 8, 10b) – allegorical figures, monsters, men-at-arms, ships, historical vignettes, fruit, flowers, and animals. In such maps, among which the masterpieces are perhaps those of the Northern Regions by Olaus Magnus (Venice, 1539) and of Bavaria by Philipp Apian (Ingolstadt, 1568), the pictorial fantasy of the Middle Ages reflowers.

A striking reaction against this extravagance accompanied the reintroduction of copperplate engraving. In Italian maps (Pl. 11, 12), borders became simple and elegant; titles and other 'memorables' were concentrated in cartouches equally sober in design; extraneous decorative or pictorial motives were banished from the face of the map, except from the sea, which was still frequented by the traditional ships and monsters, and from other 'spare and voide places' which might accommodate a patron's coat of arms or some characteristic detail such as an antiquity or astronomical instrument. The early Flemish map-makers were no less restrained. In Mercator's work (Pl. 13) almost all the decoration, except the graceful swash capitals and a few figure drawings, is concentrated on the elaborately interlaced design of the strapwork cartouche.

The expansion of the map-making industry of the Netherlands in the second half of the 16th century inaugurated the golden age of decorative cartography, which was to last until the 18th century. The technical skill of the engraving schools and competitive conditions in the map-trade combined to load maps with increasingly elaborate ornament and a wealth of pictorial detail. The formal elements in Ortelius's maps (Pl. 14–18), engraved in the Cologne workshop of Frans Hogenberg, are relatively simple: the borders are plain mouldings, the title-panels enclosed in frames of fretted and morticed woodwork 'tricked'

[1] Folkingham was mainly concerned with manuscript estate maps.

[2] But the world map in an edition of Pomponius Mela (Venice 1482) is framed in a handsome Renaissance loggia supported by four Corinthian columns.

[3] The decorative borders in the editions of Ptolemy of 1535 and 1541 are attributed to Holbein and Urs Graf.

with pendant flowers and fruit, with birds and animals, nymphs, fauns, masks, coats of arms, and other detail borrowed from Italian Renaissance ornament.[1] But over the face of the maps is scattered a profusion of little pictures: people in local costume and indigenous animals (elephants in Africa, camels in Tartary, reindeer in the Arctic, goats in Norway), vignettes of episodes from the Bible or from Marco Polo, and much else. The city atlas engraved by Hogenberg, Georg Braun's *Civitates orbis terrarum*, is equally rich in figure drawings, boldly placed in the foreground (Pl. 19–22); that this was deliberate, we learn from Braun's preface, which says that the figures were introduced not only to depict local costume and manners but also to deny his work to the Turk, who might use it against Christendom did not his religion forbid the representation of the human form! Drawn in perspective, the town plans and views engraved by Hogenberg for Braun's atlas are, of course, rich in pictorial detail, but their ornament is severe.

The decorative fashion of the Ortelius maps engraved by Hogenberg was generally adopted at the end of the 16th century. It may be seen in the work of Saxton's engravers, of whom Hogenberg's brother Remigius was one (Pl. 32–34), and in the more elaborate designs of the van Langeren and van Deutecum families at Antwerp (Pl. 27–30) and of Jodocus Hondius at Amsterdam (Pl. 43–48). Decorative cartouches, cunningly varied, now framed not only the title but also the scale, coats of arms, dedication, signature and imprint, and inset plans or pictures. For the maps of his *Theatre* (Pl. 37–40) Speed provided Hondius with a rich miscellany of illustrations – town plans, portraits and costume designs, historical pictures, drawings of buildings and antiquities, rubbings of coins, heraldic devices, descriptive legends; and we may admire the skill with which the engraver has woven them into the general design of each map, the diverse parts of which are linked by motives imitating carved or moulded wood or by ribbon-work and figures. Here too can be seen the development of the border to accommodate matter not forming part of the map itself; and this became common in the 17th century (Pl. 56).

In the next generation, engravers, spurred by commercial rivalry, became more exuberant, and throughout the century maps from the workshops of Jansson, Blaeu, Visscher, Danckerts, Goos, de Wit and many other craftsmen showed brilliant and ingenious variations on old and new decorative motives. The pictorial possibilities in map design were exploited as never before (not without detriment to geographical values), and Blaeu's atlas was described by a contemporary as a picture book for the dilettante rather than a text-book for the geographer. The new mode was well described in an English manual on design published early in the century:[2] 'You may, if you list, draw naked boys riding and playing with their paper-mils or bubble-shels upon Goates, Eagles, Dolphins &c. the bones of a Rams head hung with strings of beads and Ribands, Satyres, Tritons, Apes, Cornu-copia's, Dogs yoakt, &c. drawing Cowcumbers, Cherries, and any Kind of wild traile or vinet after your owne invention, with a thousand more such idle toyes, so that herein you cannot be too fantastical. The late Dutch peeces in this kinde excell all others.'

Cartouches were generally smaller and more naturalistic; the elaborate formal fretwork design disappeared, and they were set in strapwork frames or on shells or drapery. The supporting groups, which are of great variety and interest, include natives in local costume bearing weapons or implements of agriculture and other pursuits, allegorical and classical figures, and the innumerable cherubs, or 'putti', who haunted maps for two centuries, often holding instruments for astronomy, survey and map-drawing. The pictorial vignettes formerly scattered over the map were now more usually assembled round the cartouches or

[1] 'The Scale and Compasse', says Folkingham, '. . . may be florished with Fruitage or Imagery.'
[2] Henry Peacham, *Graphice or the . . . Art of Drawing and Limming* (1612), p. 50.

in the margins. Heraldic designs were elaborate and beautifully drawn; an extreme example is Blaeu's map of the territory of Frankfort (Pl. 59). Title-pages, especially those of sea-atlases, were luxuriantly furnished with ornament (Pl. 64).

Work from the houses of Blaeu and Danckerts was held in especially high regard by collectors of decorative maps in their own day, and the Dutch fashion was copied by carto-graphers of other countries. How indifferently this was done in England may be seen in John Seller's charts (Pl. 67). As the conventional technique of map-drawing matured in the late 17th and 18th centuries,[1] extraneous ornament (whether pictorial or formal) was more and more removed from the face of the map to the borders and panels; and it is in these that developments in design, following contemporary fashion in the applied arts, must be looked for. The baroque style, which with slight national variations prevailed in all European countries and was practised with particular mastery by the French (Pl. 79, 80), organised the frame of the cartouche as a single harmonious design, which might include trophies of arms, animal and human figures, architectural details, fruit and flowers, drapery, and the ubiquitous acanthus leaves. The cartouche on William Mayo's map of Barbados, engraved by Senex in 1722 (Pl. 84), is a good English example, perhaps influenced[2] by the wood-carvings of Grinling Gibbons. By the middle of the century the formal frames were drawn in a lighter rococo style, containing the same elements; and this in turn was supplanted by a pictorial design of trees or natural products. The decoration of 18th-century maps also followed (and indeed fostered) the contemporary vogue for *chinoiserie* (Pl. 80); and the taste for classical ruins, imaginatively interpreted by Piranesi's views of ancient Rome, was reflected in the cartouches of many English maps.

Colour

Colour has, throughout the history of printed maps, been used not only as decoration but also to supplement and distinguish the engraved symbols. The earliest map-engravers, who were often skilled miniaturists, coloured the features of their maps according to the traditional conventions of manuscript cartography, and map-makers of the next three centuries made few changes in these fashions, many of which are still in use to-day. In maps of the 15th century, as later, seas, lakes and rivers are blue, woods and meadowland green, roads yellow or brown, the roofs of houses in town symbols red or blue, mountains are shaded in brown or ochre tipped with red, countries or provinces have distinctive tints. Territorial boundaries were in fact indicated by lines of colour before a drawn or engraved symbol was devised for them.

Early printers, relying more on linear symbols than the designers of manuscript maps, could afford to be more sparing in the use of colour. When used, as in the woodcut maps popular in Central Europe in the 16th century, it was applied in a flat wash, often laid on rather densely. The Italian copper-plate engravers, conscious no doubt of the grace of their line-work, seldom added colour to it; but in the Netherlands the ancient art of illumination was adapted to the colouring of maps, which before the middle of the 16th century had become an independent trade, recognised by artists' guilds such as that of St Luke at Antwerp. Ortelius first set up in business as a 'painter of maps'; and map-engravers had their newly printed maps coloured either by illuminators employed in their own shops or by other craftsmen, such as Bernard van der Putte, who specialised in this work. From the 16th to the 18th centuries maps were advertised for sale 'coloured or plain', and copies with contemporary colouring still command the higher prices.

[1] See pp. 12–13 above.   [2] As E. Lynam has suggested.

As the decoration of Flemish and Dutch maps grew more profuse and fanciful, the colourist's opportunity became greater and his conventions more diverse. His brush was no longer restricted to the face of the map. Here indeed, as we can see from a map by Blaeu or Danckerts (Pl. 61, 73), his work became more refined in the 17th century; outline supplanted solid colours, lighter washes were used, relief features were more subtly shaded. But from the 'complements and compartiments' of the Dutch maps colours blazed in brilliant variety. The fretwork tracery or strapwork of the formal cartouches of the 16th century was usually done in magenta or brown, picked out with gold, blue and many other colours. The more naturalistic ornament introduced in the 17th century – trophies, cornucopias, cherubs, groups of figures, ribbons, fruit and flowers – was 'coloured according to the nature of it', as John Smith tells us,[1] instancing '*Crowns*, or anything representing Gold with Yellow . . . the Hair of Men or Women with Tincture of *Myrrh* . . . the Flesh of Women or Boys, with a very little of the Tincture of *Cochinele*, in a large Quantity of Water, and Garments either with thin Green shadowed with thicker . . . or with *Vermillion* shaded with *Carmine*'. Coats of arms were brightly blazoned and gilded, compass-roses and scales painted in gay variety. Vignettes and the little pictures of people and animals, instruments and tools, ships and sea-monsters all had characteristic colouring. For ships, Smith recommends 'painting the Hull . . . with *Umber*, the Sails with Tincture of *Myrrh*, and the Flags with *Vermillion* or *Blue Bice*; and if they are represented as firing their Guns, let all the *Smoak* be done with very thin *Bice*'. The border of the maps had its special conventions: 'as for the Margent, or square stick of Degrees . . . which goes round the map, let that be coloured either with Yellow or Red-lead, or Crimson, none but those three Colours serving well for this purpose'.

The illumination of Dutch maps was universally admired; 'the only way to colour Maps well', says John Smith, 'is by a pattern done by some good Workman, of which the Dutch are esteemed the best'. The chapter on 'the whole Art and Mystery of Colouring Maps . . . with Water Colours' which he added to the third impression of his book in 1701, gives a vivid account of contemporary conventions.[2] The illuminator is instructed first to wash over the hills with tincture of myrrh; then to do every tree with grass green applied on the point of a fine pencil, and cities and towns with red lead; to outline boundaries, 'Known by certain Lines, or Rows of Pricks, or Points of several Sizes and Shapes', in contrasted colours, taking care to 'miss' hills, woods and towns; to colour water with thin indigo, and land (if coloured) with a very thin yellow or light green wash.

Yet, when Smith wrote, the elaboration and multiplication of conventional signs was already driving colour from the face of the map. It continued to blaze in borders, cartouches, coats of arms, and other 'compartiments' of the map, but 18th-century cartographers were reluctant to let it obscure their numerous and subtly differentiated symbols. When applied to physical features, as in Cassini's map of the environs of Paris (Pl. 81), it was laid on thinly. More often it was retained only for outlining boundaries and coasts, although smaller-scale maps (as to-day) commonly spread distinctive tints over the whole area of adjoining countries or provinces.

But colour is little less essential a part of the cartographer's vocabulary than conventional signs. Geographers of the 18th century who defined maps as 'paintings' did not refer only to their decoration. Gregorii in 1713, for instance, described a map as 'a painting in which the earth or parts of it are artistically represented on a flat surface'. Colour as a means of representing geographical facts, especially those of relief, came into its own again in the 19th century with the introduction of colour printing.

[1] John Smith, *The Art of Painting in Oyl* (1701), p. 106.
[2] Smith, pp. 103–110. J. G. Gregorii, in his *Curieuse Gedancken* (1713), chap. xii, also describes the technique.

The publishers of maps, as of books, have not seldom — and not only in our own day — been guilty of the commercial discourtesy of failing to date their wares. As the writer of a leader in *The Times* sharply remarked a few years ago, 'undated maps . . . can be a delusion and a snare, especially in these days of the violent removal of landmarks all over the world'. Early maps bearing no date may be no less misleading to the collector or historian.

The early mapseller's carelessness in recording the date and place of printing or publication sprang mainly from the conditions of printing from copper plates and from the organisation of the map-trade. Letterpress type, reset for a new printing, offers tell-tale clues which can be easily detected; but impressions could be pulled from a copper plate many years after engraving, without alteration of the inked surface. Plates passed, by sale or inheritance, from the stock of one publisher to that of another, who often reprinted from them without correcting the date, the imprint, or the geographical content of the map.

Let us look at the history of John Speed's map of Surrey (Pl. 38) to illustrate the problem of dating an isolated impression. If our copy of the map was printed in one of the editions of the *Theatre* published between 1611 and 1676, it will have printed text on the back (and will show signs of having been folded down the middle); the state of the text, which was newly set eight times,[1] will provide some help in dating, but we must remember that many reissues of the atlas were made by printing new impressions of the maps (which might meanwhile have been altered on the plates) on the back of letterpress pages set up and run off earlier.[2]

After examining the watermark, which may date the impression within some 20—30 years, we turn to the face of the map. This is, of course, our only resource if the map has no text on the back; in this case it must have been printed for sale either as a separate sheet,[3] or in one of the 'setts of maps' sold in the late 17th and 18th centuries, or in one of the two 18th-century editions.[4] The original plate of Surrey, completed by Hondius in 1610, bore the engraver's signature and date ('Jodocus Hondius cælavit. Anno 1610') and the map-sellers' imprint and privilege ('Are to be solde . . . by John Sudbury and George Humble Cum privilegio').[5] Minor corrections or additions were made on the map for editions of the *Theatre* in 1614 and 1623; by 1627 a corner of the plate had broken off, and by 1631 it had been repaired; for the 1662 edition of the *Theatre* the original imprint was deleted and that of 'Roger Rea the Elder and Younger' substituted; and in the 1676 edition this was in turn displaced by the imprint of Thomas Bassett and Richard Chiswell. The plate, although it was meanwhile owned and printed by two other mapsellers,[6] was not again altered until after 1707, when (with the other Speed plates) it came into the possession of Henry Overton; between this date and 1743, when he published his atlas, Overton added roads to the map, inserted his own imprint, and last of all removed the date 1610. Finally, by about 1770 the imprint of Dicey and Co. had been substituted for Overton's.

From this brief history of the Surrey plate, we can see how limited and unreliable is the evidence provided by the printed surface of the map. It only betrays the state of the plate at the time of printing; it does not necessarily tell us much about the date of impression or the circumstances of printing. Two of the mapsellers who owned the plate of Surrey and sold impressions from it never put their imprint on it; and the original date '1610' remained on the plate until nearly 1743. Nor is the geographical content of the Surrey map very

---

[1] For the editions of 1611, 1614, 1616 (the only Latin edition), 1627, 1631, 1646, 1662, and 1676.

[2] See above, p. 4. At least five reissues of the 1646 text (all with the date 1650 on the title-page) are known; each of these has one or more maps in a revised state.

[3] Separate impressions, with blank backs, were sold throughout the long career of Speed's plates.

[4] Henry Overton's of 1743, or C. Dicey's of about 1770; both without text.

[5] An earlier proof, of which two impressions are known, lacks these and many other details.

[6] Christopher Browne and John Overton.

helpful. Speed copied it from Norden's map of 1594, inserting the hundreds and some place-names; and, with the exception of corrections and additions made in his lifetime (i.e. before 1629), and of a few more place-names engraved for the 1676 edition, no change appeared in the map until Henry Overton added the roads (from Ogilby's road-atlas) about 1720. Thus the topography in Dicey's map of 1770, although three important surveys of the county had been made in the preceding hundred years, is substantially that of Norden's survey of the late 16th century.

Plainly we must distinguish between evidence relating to (*a*) the impression, and (*b*) the engraving or latest revision of the plate. The date of printing may be determined – not infallibly, as we have seen – from the state of the plate; the name and address of the map-seller, contemporary heraldry, or a dedication to a living patron – any of these may at least provide a *terminus post quem*[1] for the impression. More reliable is the make of paper used,[2] which can be approximately dated by identifying its watermark in one of the great specimen books: C. M. Briquet's *Les Filigranes* (1907) for papers before 1600, or Edward Heawood's *Watermarks* (1950) for 17th- and 18th-century papers, especially English. A separate map, backed by text, from an atlas can be more precisely dated in the 16th century, when (for instance) the text of Ortelius's *Theatrum* was substantially reset for each new edition, than in the 17th, when Jansson or Blaeu reprinted their atlas-maps many times with one setting of their text. Finally, different impressions from an unaltered plate can be placed in chronological order by noticing progressive wear of the engraved surface, the appearance of cracks or fractures in the plate,[3] or signs of reworking or repair. All these clues, taken from the impression itself, may be supplemented or confirmed by external evidence: a contemporary reference to the printing of the map, a mapseller's catalogue or advertisement, or an entry in trade lists such as (for England) the Stationers' Register or the 'Term Catalogues'.[4]

The history of Speed's map of Surrey shows with what caution the printed surface of a map must be used in dating the engraver's work on the plate. Some information about the plate in its original state may be drawn from the signatures of the cartographer and engraver, from the mapseller's imprint, or from the style of lettering, of decoration, and of the conventional signs. A mapseller may sometimes leave a helpful clue, as when Richard Blome substitutes a new for an old patron's coat of arms on his map of the Channel Islands (first printed in 1673); more often he is misleading. The geographical facts in a map are most suspect of all the evidence for dating it. Anachronism is common. A cartographer cannot draw details unknown to him, but he can – and frequently did – omit information known to him or to his contemporaries. We may accordingly assign to a map a *terminus post quem* from what it includes, but are not justified in inferring a *terminus ante quem*[5] from what it omits. A map which draws New Zealand as two islands, separated by Cook Strait, must be later than Captain Cook's first voyage (1768–71); a map showing only the west coast, with no strait, must be later than Tasman (1642) but may be later than Cook. Mapsellers were

---

[1] The earliest date at which the map could have been printed.

[2] If, as is usual, the map is printed on paper, and not on vellum or less commonly used materials (e.g. satin).

[3] Three distinct editions of the miniature atlas *England Wales Scotland and Ireland described*, published by George Humble, are all dated 1627 on the engraved title-page and have the same plates (in the same state) but with different settings of the text. Dr Harold Whitaker has placed these in correct order by noting the growth of cracks in certain maps. The true dates of printing are thought to be 1627, 1632 and 1646.

[4] The Registers of the Stationers' Company have been printed for the years 1557–1708; the 'Term Catalogues', a reprint of a trade journal called *Mercurius Librarius*, for 1668–1711. The former seldom, the latter generally, record maps as well as books.

[5] The latest date at which a map could have been made.

often guilty of obstinate resistance to new facts. The ideas of 16th- and 17th-century carto-graphers on the sources of the Nile, which they placed south of the Equator, were corrected by H. Ludolf (from Jesuit reports) in his map of Abyssinia of 1683; yet nearly fifty years later the Nuremberg mapseller J. B. Homann not only reproduced the discredited version but warned his readers that 'Ludolf has hitherto been followed by unwary geographers who have misrepresented the source of the Nile on recent maps'.

No less caution is needed in accepting the dates on engraved title-pages of atlases. Here Speed may again provide an illustration. The same plate served as the title-page for all editions of the *Theatre* with text, except the last (1676); for this a new plate, copied from the old, was engraved. The date was regularly corrected until the 1627 edition, but was only once again altered before 1676, although three further editions and numerous reissues were published.[1] If we examine the edition of 1631, we find the dates 1627 on the engraved title-page; 1631 on the letterpress title-pages of books II–IV; 1632 on the map of England (from a new plate); and 1631 on the title-page of the companion volume, Speed's *Prospect of the most Famous Parts of the World*. The date on an engraved title-page should always be verified by comparison with type-printed dates in the text (especially in a dedication, preface, or additional title-page) and with engraved dates on the maps.

VII. THE MORTALITY OF MAPS

Like other written or printed records, many early maps have perished in the catastrophes to which human affairs are subject. Of these, fire and war have been the most destructive.

The Great Fire of London in 1666 ravaged the centres of the book and print trades about Newgate and St Paul's, and Pepys tells us that £150,000 worth of stock was lost. Although the official list of printers 'disabled by ye fire'[2] includes no map-dealers, it is clear from indirect evidence that both plates and printed stocks of maps were destroyed. New editions of Saxton's and Speed's atlases projected in or about 1665 were never completed or published, and by 1689, when Philip Lea issued an edition of Saxton's atlas, the plates of Devonshire and Northumberland had disappeared.[3] The scarcity of maps and atlases printed within a few years before the Fire[4] can be explained only by the destruction of the sheets in the printshops. On 22 February 1672 Joan Blaeu's famous house on the Blumen-gracht at Amsterdam was burned down, with its equipment, some (but not all) of the Blaeu plates, and a large number of printed sheets, including those of the great 12-volume Spanish edition of the *Atlas Major* (of which only ten volumes had been completed). Very few copies of this rare edition are known; but Blaeu partly made good his loss by pasting leaves of the Spanish letterpress over the text pages of the Dutch or French edition, and copies are found in this form.[5] We are told some forty years later[6] that because of the fire Blaeu's atlas had 'become so rare that it is found only in a few libraries of kings and princes', and that copies were to be had in Amsterdam only at high prices.

The tale of disaster is long and melancholy, and should include the Lisbon earthquake of 1751, when the greater part of the Portuguese Archives were lost, and the two world wars of the 20th century. In the first of these, many old maps were destroyed with the library of

---

[1] The title-page with date 1627 is found in the editions of 1627, 1631, and 1646; with date 1650, in five reissues of the 1646 text (1650–54) and in the edition of 1662.

[2] Printed by H. R. Plomer, *A Short History of English Printing* (1915), p. 186.

[3] See H. Whitaker in *Imago Mundi*, III (1939), pp. 73–4.

[4] Such as Rea's edition of Speed's *Theatre* and his miniature atlas, both of 1662.

[5] E.g. in the British Museum and the Mitchell Library, Glasgow.

[6] By J. G. Gregorii, in *Curieuse Gedancken von . . . Alt- und Neuen Landcharten* (1713). This book is a mine of discursive information on 17th-century maps.

Louvain University; the catalogue of losses in the second is not yet complete, but is known to include many treasures in Germany and Italy, notably the great medieval mappamundi of Ebstorf (1284) and that of Giovanni da Carignano (*c.* 1300).[1]

Such catastrophes alone do not explain the high mortality of old maps and the small proportion of survivors. The materials for the history of cartography are fragmentary. Maps are in the first instance tools for practical men. Pilots, travellers, soldiers, engineers need new maps, and discard them as soon as they have exhausted their usefulness or no longer reflect current knowledge. Hard use, while they are still serviceable, and neglect, when they have ceased to be, are the principal enemies of maps. Only in 'the libraries of kings and princes', of dilettanti and scholars who valued old maps for their decorative beauty, their historical interest, their strangeness, or simply their antiquity, have they had any chance of preservation. This belongs to the history of collecting, which is considered in the next section.

The physical character of maps is discouraging to their survival. They are usually drawn or printed on perishable materials;[2] like other unbound broadsides, they are not protected by covers; they present awkward problems of storage, especially when they are large. Maps have been carved or drawn on stone, made in mosaic or painted in fresco, worked in tapestry, cut, cast or stamped in different metals; but the materials commonly used as their base have been vellum and (from about the 14th century) paper. Vellum has the virtues of durability and of a hard surface which takes ink and colour with greater brilliance; it has accordingly been preferred by cartographers for maps specially subject to hard wear (such as pilots' charts), for splendidly produced copies for patrons or collectors,[3] and for maps drawn as legal records[4] or as state papers. Paper, as the cheaper material, has been more generally used for map-printing; and for impressions from copper plates, especially if they were to be coloured, specially fine and thick paper was recommended.[5]

Although the multiplication of copies by the press might be expected to reduce the risk of loss, many printed maps have totally vanished or have survived in few copies, often only one. Of some now lost maps we have notices in contemporary records, such as Ortelius's correspondence or Plantin's account-books; others can only be guessed at, and hitherto unknown maps turn up not infrequently. The list on the opposite page (which is far from exhaustive) indicates the rarity of some important printed maps of the 16th and 17th centuries.

Most of these are big wall maps printed from a number of plates or blocks – a form which was specially popular in Central and Western Europe. Although printed in large editions (1,000 copies of Waldseemuller's map of 1507, and certainly not fewer of most of the others listed), maps of this type were most liable to destruction or deterioration. They

---

[1] An early inventory (1575) of maps bequeathed to the Louvain library was printed by L. Bagrow in *Imago Mundi*, V (1948), pp. 18–20. Lists of losses in World War II, under the title 'With fire and sword', have appeared in *Imago Mundi*, IV–VI (1947–49).

[2] The English term 'map', first recorded in 1527, is derived (through the medieval 'mappamundi') from a Latin word meaning a cloth or napkin; 'chart' ('card' or 'carte' in the 16th century) from the Greek word for a papyrus leaf.

[3] To this class belong many of the surviving 'portolan' charts from the 14th to 17th centuries, and the large mappaemundi of the late Middle Ages; a magnificent example is the Catalan World Map presented to King Charles V of France in 1375. Among printed examples may be mentioned the only known copy of Saxton's atlas on vellum (now in the Library of Congress).

[4] Estate maps and terriers are commonly drawn on vellum.

[5] 'If your Paper be good and bear the Colours well, without suffering them to sink into it, all . . . will lie fair and pleasant to the Eye . . . but if the Paper be not good and strong, no Art can make the Colours lie well; therefore in buying *Maps*, chuse those that are Printed on the strongest or thickest Paper.' (John Smith, *The Art of Painting in Oyl*, 1701, p. 110.)

were too large to be framed and glazed; if rolled or hung they were subject to risks of tearing, cracking, abrasion, and dirt; and they often survive only as library copies in which separate sheets have been bound up as an atlas. This is the form in which, for instance, Waldsee-müller's two world maps, one copy of Saxton's large map, and the Blaeu map of 1618 have been preserved.

	Number of copies extant
Contarini-Rosselli, world map, 1506	1
Waldseemüller, world map, 1507	1
Waldseemüller, Europe, 1511	None; only a later edition of 1520 is known
Waldseemüller, Carta marina, 1516	1
Mercator, Palestine, 1537	1
Mercator, world map, 1538	2
Mercator, Flanders, 1540	1
Mercator, Europe, 1554	1
Mercator, British Isles, 1564	3
Mercator, world chart, 1569	4
Saxton, England and Wales, 1583	2
Plancius, world map, 1592	1
Plancius, world map, 1604	1
Blaeu, world map, 1605	1
Hondius, world map, 1608	1
Blaeu, world map, 1618	1

To-day atlases are too commonly broken up by dealers, who can obtain better prices for the maps as separate sheets; this butchery has made many atlases, in their original form, needlessly scarce.

VIII. THE HISTORY OF MAP-COLLECTING

The taste for collecting and studying old maps, like other antiquities, may be justified by Dr Johnson's remark: 'Whatever withdraws us from the power of our senses, whatever makes the past, the distant, or the future predominate over the present, advances us in the dignity of thinking beings.' Yet map-making is a practical art, and Johnson himself advised King George III's librarian on the formation of the King's cabinet of contemporary maps and plans. It was as reference libraries of current or 'modern' cartography that many surviving collections of early maps were assembled by their founders.[1]

The Renaissance of the 15th and 16th centuries encouraged the cult of classical antiquity in Western Europe, where men began deliberately to search for and to preserve its relics. It was, however, not as an 'antique' but as a systematic representation of the contemporary world that the maps of Ptolemy were recovered, printed and acclaimed. The expansion of the known world by the great discoveries brought later cartographers a mass of new material, and their work was useful to geographers only if it was up-to-date. For the compilation of

[1] Yet even into these, maps already old found their way; for instance, the library of Pepys's patron William Legge, first Earl of Dartmouth, contained not only the drafts of Charles II's hydrographers and engineers, but also a chart by William Borough which was a hundred years older, and other Elizabethan military and naval sketches. The collection was dispersed by sale at Sotheby's on 9 March 1948; and the Borough chart is now in the National Maritime Museum, Greenwich.

atlases, from its tentative beginnings in Italy to the triumphant enterprise of Ortelius, collections of source material had to be formed; Ortelius's letters tell the story of his anxious search through Europe for the best modern maps of all parts of the world, and the prototype of his atlas was a collection of maps by other cartographers of his day.[1]

However, as the art of cartography developed, the interest of *virtuosi* extended from the manuscript map, with whose fine craftsmanship they had long been familiar, to the printed map 'to beautify their Halls, Parlors, Chambers, Galeries, Studies or Libraries with'; and it was of printed maps, still current in his day, that Robert Burton wrote 'What greater pleasure can there now be than to view those elaborate Maps of Ortelius, Mercator, Hondius, &c. To peruse those books of Cities, put out by Braunus and Hogenbergius?'[2] Maps were, however, sought not only as decorative works of art, but also as historical records or (as we should now say) sources for historical geography. In the search for ancient manuscripts made by humanists and antiquaries of the 15th and 16th centuries, old maps were rescued, studied and reproduced. Konrad Peutinger, classical scholar and town clerk of Nuremberg in the early 16th century, brought to light a map of Central Europe drawn fifty years earlier by Cardinal Nicholas of Cusa, and had it engraved. His friend Konrad Celtes discovered a road map of the Roman world[3] in a library at Worms and left it to Peutinger, whose name it has since borne. The 'Tabula Peutingeriana', or Peutinger Table, was engraved in 1591, and this is perhaps the first example of the reproduction of an old map, as such, by printing.[4] Into the hands of English 16th-century antiquaries came many manuscript maps from the libraries of dissolved religious houses, and the collections of Archbishop Matthew Parker (bequeathed to Corpus Christi College, Cambridge) and Sir Robert Cotton (now in the British Museum) contained *inter alia* nearly all the maps made by Matthew Paris at St Albans in the 14th century. William Camden and John Speed drew liberally on Cotton's treasures, and Speed paid tribute to 'the worthy repairer of eating times ruines, the learned Sir Robert Cotté ... whose Cabinets were unlocked, & Library ... set open to my free accesse'.[5]

Cartography and historical studies were near allies in the 16th century, when the historical atlas made its appearance as a set of maps of the ancient world. The historical map, in particular the Biblical map, was not a new form; in the Middle Ages maps of the Holy Land were drawn to indicate the divisions of the Twelve Tribes, and Matthew Paris's manuscripts contain a map of Roman roads in Britain and a diagram of the Anglo-Saxon kingdoms. Ortelius, himself a dealer in antiquities, added to later editions of his *Theatrum* (from 1579) an increasing number of 'ancient' maps under the title *Parergon Theatri*. The *Parergon*, the last edition of which (1624) contained 49 maps including the Peutinger Table, was the forerunner of the elaborate classical atlases which from the middle of the 17th century formed a volume in the great compilations of Jansson and Blaeu. In England, antiquaries of the 16th century were the pioneers of topographical studies: John Leland 'our British Pausanias',[6] Laurence Nowell the Anglo-Saxon scholar, William Lambard the historian of Kent, William Camden, Cotton, Speed, John Stow, and others. Nowell's maps of the British Isles[7] have Anglo-Saxon place-names, and Camden drew a map of Anglo-Saxon England which was copied by Speed (Pl. 37).

[1] See p. 46 below.
[2] Robert Burton, *Anatomy of Melancholy*, pt. 2, sect. 2, member 4.
[3] Of the third century A.D.; but the copy found by Celtes was made in the 13th century.
[4] If we exclude Ptolemy's maps.
[5] Speed, *History of Great Britaine* (1627), Summary Conclusion.
[6] As Richard Gough called him.
[7] In the Cotton manuscripts at the British Museum, MS. Domitian XVIII. 13.

Although few old maps were found to support these speculative reconstructions of ancient geography, their value to the historian was appreciated by collectors and antiquaries of the 17th and 18th centuries. Samuel Pepys collected not only London plans and views of all periods, but also early charts to illustrate his projected history of the English Navy, and his care for them appears in many passages of his diary.[1] In the 18th century the hunt for early maps and enquiry into their history grew wider and deeper. As early as 1713 Gregorii wrote that they had 'become so rare that they are not easily met with. They are as precious as old coins.' At about this time Thomas Hearne was searching Oxford libraries for old maps, and booksellers were reprinting Norden's manuscript surveys. By the middle of the century the most famous of all forged maps – the supposed map and Itinerary of Roman Britain by Richard of Cirencester – had been produced by Charles Bertram, of Copenhagen, to feed the demand for early maps among English antiquaries. To the same period belongs Richard Gough's contribution, the greatest in this and perhaps in any country, to the methodical study of early maps. His *British Topography* (1780) is still an indispensable reference book; and among his topographical collections, now in the Bodleian library, are preserved many notable maps.[2]

Although by Gough's day, as he tells us, 'many capital collections of MSS. have been dispersed irrecoverably' and his notes record not a few lost maps, dilettanti were in fact collecting early maps with growing activity and discrimination. Among English private libraries of the 18th century rich in this kind of material were those of Sir Hans Sloane (acquired for the British Museum on its foundation in 1753), of Joseph Smith the British consul in Venice (purchased by George III in 1762), of Richard Rawlinson (bequeathed to the Bodleian on his death in 1755), and many others. These were the forerunners of the majestic private collections formed in the 19th century, among which those of James Lenox and John Carter Brown in America, of Jomard and Nordenskiöld in Europe, rank high for their judicious selection, wealth of material, and usefulness to scholars; all four are now in public ownership.

In the end, as Gough remarked, 'a public library is the safest port'; and the national libraries of most European countries contain the collections of princes and statesmen who had both the opportunity and the need to assemble the best contemporary maps at all periods. Few such collections have, like that of Lord Burghley still at Hatfield House, remained in the families of their founders. Until the 18th century royal map collectors still led their private rivals; 'the great atlases', wrote Gregorii in 1713, 'are to be found in the libraries of kings and princes, because they are much too costly for a private individual'.

Before the modern organisation of departmental archives, the royal cabinet was the natural repository for maps produced by servants of the state: military engineers, naval hydrographers, topographical surveyors employed by the Government. Abroad, ambassadors and other agents were commissioned to buy maps for the King's private collection. Plantin's ledgers record the maps and instruments which from 1558 to 1588 he supplied to Benito Arias Montano (Montanus) for the account of King Philip II, whose library is now in the Escorial; and a set of Italian maps assembled in 1568 for his master by Don Luis Hurtado de Toledo, Spanish Ambassador in Venice, is now in an American collection.[3]

[1] E.g. 19 September 1666: 'mightily troubled, and even in my sleep at my missing . . . Speeds Chronicle and Maps, and the two parts of Waggoner [Waghenaer], and a book of cards, which I suppose I have put up with too much care that I have forgot where they are'. His splendid collection now belongs to his Cambridge college, Magdalene.

[2] Including the famous 'Gough-Bodleian' road map of Great Britain, drawn probably in the first half of the 14th century.

[3] That of Mr George H. Beans, Philadelphia. See his pamphlet *A Collection of Maps compiled by Luis Hurtado de Toledo* (1943).

On his accession in 1660 Charles II was presented by J. Klencke and other Amsterdam merchants with a gigantic atlas, measuring in its binding 5 ft. 10 in. by 3 ft. 2 in. and containing 42 large maps by Dutch engravers.[1] The Klencke atlas is among the 'super-atlases' (as Wieder called them), often of Amsterdam origin, which found their way into kings' libraries in the heyday of royal collecting. The 'Atlas Royal', compiled at Amsterdam, 1706–10, for Augustus the Strong, King of Saxony, contains 1,400 maps in 19 volumes; a 24-volume collection of Dutch maps and town-plans made in 1718 by Christoffel Beudeker, of Amsterdam, is now in the British Museum; and the greatest of all, the Blaeu *Atlas Major* extended to 46 volumes by Laurens van der Hem in the 17th century, was acquired in 1730 by Prince Eugene of Savoy and from him, in 1737, by the Austrian royal library.[2]

The sovereign who made perhaps the most remarkable use of his opportunities for collecting maps was George III of England. His father had in 1757 transferred to the British Museum the Old Royal Library accumulated since the 15th century, and on his accession in 1760 George III began to form a new collection, in which geography and topography were to be conspicuous. Maps were gathered from military and civil surveys, charts from the work of official hydrographers; topographical material was sought wherever it was to be had, abroad and at home. After 60 years the King's Librarian could write: 'The Collections of Geography and Topography . . . have increased to an extent not hitherto equalled; and the Collection of Military Plans is of the greatest value and importance.'[3] These collections, rich not only in contemporary but also in early maps, are now in the British Museum.

To-day, collectors of early maps are probably more numerous than ever before. Served by a growing literature on their subject they are also better informed and more exacting. But the days of easy opportunity and low prices are almost gone. In the past twenty or thirty years commercial values have risen steeply, and in booksellers' catalogues and auction rooms the prices of famous atlases and sheet-maps have multiplied two-, three-, and even ten-fold. When we see the 1513 Ptolemy realising £450, the *Civitates* of Braun and Hogenberg £600, single maps by Saxton from £5 to £20, Speed's *Theatre* of 1611–12 £300 or more, Dudley's *Arcano* £1,000, and Blaeu's *Atlas Major* £750, it is evident that, for such works, the student and connoisseur must become increasingly dependent on public collections. Yet many interesting and significant maps may still be had at moderate prices; and if the great 'finds' of the past will hardly be repeated, luck supported by expertise may still bring together a considerable and even valuable collection, particularly in fields and periods which are still unfamiliar or held in low esteem by contemporary fashion.

[1] Now in the British Museum, which has a contemporary MS. catalogue of Charles II's maps (Royal MSS., App. 86).
[2] See F. C. Wieder, *Monumenta Cartographica*, v (1933).
[3] *Bibliothecae Regiae Catalogus*, vol i.

General Bibliography

COMPREHENSIVE BIBLIOGRAPHY would fill a substantial volume. The following list is designed only to illustrate some classes of reference material that will serve further inquiry into the topics of this book, and to note, as examples, a few of the more useful works in each category. It may be supplemented by the short lists attached to the eight chapters which follow.

Numerous articles on individual maps, groups of maps, or cartographers are to be found in periodicals of a geographical, historical, or archaeological character. Their titles may be collected from bibliographies in the works listed below, and in particular from the bibliographical record which appears regularly in *Imago Mundi*.

Plans for a general history of cartography have, since the early 18th century, been numerous, but in nearly every case richer in promise than in performance. All the attempted histories, except that of L. Bagrow (1951), deal with a part of the subject only, or approach it with a special bias that defeats their purpose.

History of cartography: general works

L. BAGROW (ed.), *Imago Mundi. A periodical review of early cartography* (1935–51, etc.). The only periodical devoted wholly to the history of maps. Published annually.

L. BAGROW, *Die Geschichte der Kartographie* (1951). The only objective history of early maps which fulfils its promise.

L. A. BROWN, *The story of maps* (1949). A discursive work which, in spite of its title, deals more fully with the historical and scientific circumstances of map-making than with the maps themselves. Nonetheless a mine of useful information.

R. V. TOOLEY, *Maps and map-making* (1949). A factual and bibliographical account of early maps to the 19th century. Although not a history, this contains much useful reference material, including excellent summary lists, e.g. of editions of early atlases, English county maps, etc. The reprint of 1952 contains an additional chapter on Scandinavia.

SIR H. G. FORDHAM, *Maps, their history, characteristics, and uses* (1921).

I. J. CURNOW, *The world mapped* (1930).

E. L. STEVENSON, *Terrestrial and celestial globes* (1921).

M. FIORINI, *Sfere terrestri e celesti* (1898).
    The two standard works on early globes.

A. LAUSSEDAT, *Recherches sur les instruments, les méthodes et le dessin topographiques* (1898–1903). Contains a valuable discussion of the technique of representation in maps.

E. R. KIELY, *Surveying instruments, their history and classroom use* (1947).

Among general works on cartography which contain sections on early maps, the following may be cited:

M. ECKERT, *Die Kartenwissenschaft* (1921–5).

E. A. REEVES, *Maps and map-making* (1910). With special reference to the techniques of survey and representation.

A. R. HINKS, *Maps and survey* (5th ed., 1944).

E. RAISZ, *General cartography* (2nd ed., 1948).

Bibliographies and catalogues

Bibliographies will be found in most of the works listed in other categories, particularly in that of regional cartography. Catalogues, both of public and private collections, are numerous, and (although inconsistent in quality) many are indispensable works of reference. Trade catalogues are also an important class, not only those of mapsellers of the 16th to 18th centuries, but also those of modern dealers. A few standard works in bibliographical form are noted here as specimens:

P. A. TIELE, *Nederlandsche bibliographie van land- en volkenkunde* (1884). Includes notices of atlases.

P. L. PHILLIPS, *A list of geographical atlases in the Library of Congress, with bibliographical notes* (1909–20). An invaluable reference book, with many useful bibliographical lists.

W. RUGE, 'Aelteres kartographisches Material in deutschen Bibliotheken', in *Nachrichten der K. Gesellschaft der Wissenschaften zu Göttingen, Phil.-hist. Klasse* (1904–16).

L. BAGROW, *Abrahami Ortelii catalogus cartographorum* (1928–30). Studies of the map-makers in the catalogue prefixed to Ortelius's *Theatrum* (1570). Essential for the 16th century.

L. BAGROW, 'Essay of a catalogue of map-incunabula,' in *Imago Mundi*, vii (1950).

The bibliographical section of *Imago Mundi* lists current writings on early maps; and P. L. PHILLIPS has a long (but unclassified) 'Bibliography of cartography' in his *List of maps of America* (1901). BAGROW *Geschichte* (1951), gives an excellent classified bibliography.

Some facsimile atlases

This section includes examples of both general and regional collections. It excludes such important works as those of LELEWEL (1850) and SANTAREM (1849–52), which contain mainly facsimiles of MS. maps, and also reproductions of single maps.

GENERAL

E. F. JOMARD, *Les monuments de la géographie* (1854–62). Lithographic copies of early maps in the original size and colours. A list of the maps is given by Phillips, i, 71–3.

A. E. NORDENSKIÖLD, *Facsimile atlas to the early history of cartography* (1889). Indispensable for the study of the Ptolemy editions and for the development of 'modern' cartography in the 15th and 16th centuries. A list of the facsimiles is given by Phillips, i, 75–6.

A. E. NORDENSKIÖLD, *Periplus. An essay on the early history of charts and sailing directions* (1897). A list of the facsimiles is given by Phillips, i, 77–8.

F. MULLER, *Remarkable maps of the XVth, XVIth and XVIIth centuries reproduced in their original size* (1894–7).

F. C. WIEDER, *Monumenta cartographica* (1925–33). Reproductions, in original size, of the work of cartographers of the Netherlands, 16th–17th centuries.

BRITISH MUSEUM, *Six early printed maps* (1928).

G. CARACI, *Tabulae geographicae vetustiores in Italia adservatae* (1926–32).

R. ALMAGIÀ, *Monumenta cartographica Vaticana* (1944–49, etc.).

REGIONAL

R. ALMAGIÀ, *Monumenta Italiae cartographica* (1929).

K. KRETSCHMER, *Die Entdeckung Amerikas* (atlas, 1892).

G. MARCEL, *Reproductions de cartes et globes relatives à la découverte de l'Amérique* (1893).

E. L. STEVENSON, *Maps illustrating early discovery and exploration in America* (1903–6).

E. D. FITE and A. FREEMAN, *A book of old maps delineating American history . . . to the close of the Revolutionary War* (1926).

J. F. GUILLÉN Y TATO, *Monumenta chartographica Indiana* (1942, etc.).

DUQUE DE ALBA (and others), *Mapas españoles de América, siglos XV–XVI* (1951).

PRINCE YOUSSOUF KAMAL, *Monumenta cartographica Africae et Aegypti* (1926–39, etc.).

P. TELEKI, *Atlas zur Geschichte der Kartographie der japanischen Inseln* (1909).

Some regional works

Studies or lists of the maps of particular countries, regions or towns are extremely numerous. Only a small selection is given here; others are cited among facsimile atlases.

ITALY

G. MARINELLI, *Saggio di cartografia della regione veneta* (1881).

G. MARINELLI, *Saggio di cartografia italiana* (1893).

G. UZIELLI and P. AMAT DI SAN FILIPPO, *Studi biografici e bibliografici sulla storia della geografia in Italia* (1882).

R. ALMAGIÀ, *Monumenta Italiae cartographica* (1929).

GERMANY

J. G. DOPPELMAYR, *Historische Nachricht von den Nürnbergischen Mathematicis und Künstlern* (1730).

L. GALLOIS, *Les géographes allemands de la Renaissance* (1890).

H. PRAESENT, *Beiträge zur deutschen Kartographie* (1921).

W. WOLKENHAUER, 'Deutschland im Kartenbilde', in *Deutsche geographische Blätter*, xxxix (1919–25).

E. LEHMANN, *Alte deutsche Landkarten* (1935).

A. HERRMANN, *Die ältesten Karten Deutschlands* (1940).

SWITZERLAND

L. WEISZ, *Die Schweiz auf alten Karten* (1945).

T. ISCHL, *Die ältesten Karten der Eidgenossenschaft* (1945).

FRANCE

G. ATKINSON, *La littérature géographique française de la Renaissance* (1927).

SIR H. G. FORDHAM, *Studies in carto-bibliography, British and French* (1914).

SIR H. G. FORDHAM, *Some notable surveyors & map-makers of the 16th, 17th, & 18th centuries and their work* (1929).

C. SANDLER, *Die Reformation der Kartographie um 1700* (1905).

H. M. BERTHAUT, *La carte de France, 1750–1898* (1898–9).

H. M. BERTHAUT, *Les ingénieurs géographes militaires, 1624–1831* (1902).

NETHERLANDS

P. A. TIELE, *Nederlandsche bibliographie van land- en volkenkunde* (1884).

H. E. WAUWERMANS, *Histoire de l'école cartographique belge et anversoise du XVIe siècle* (1895).

J. DENUCÉ, *Oudnederlandsche kaartmakers in betrekking met Plantijn* (1912).

F. C. WIEDER, *Nederlandsche historisch-geographische documenten in Spanje* (1915).

S. J. FOCKEMA ANDREAE and B. VAN'T HOFF, *Geschiedenis der kartografie van Nederlanden* (1947).

J. KEUNING, 'Dutch cartography in the XVIth century', in *Imago Mundi*, IX (1952).

BRITISH ISLES

R. GOUGH, *British Topography* (1780). With sections on maps.

A. L. HUMPHREYS, *A hand-book to county bibliography* (1917).

SIR H. G. FORDHAM, *Hand-list of catalogues and works of reference relating to carto-bibliography and kindred subjects for Great Britain and Ireland, 1720 to 1927* (1928).

SIR H. G. FORDHAM, *Studies in carto-bibliography, British and French* (1914).

SIR H. G. FORDHAM, *Some notable surveyors & map-makers of the 16th, 17th, & 18th centuries* (1929).

SIR H. G. FORDHAM, *The road-books & itineraries of Great Britain, 1570 to 1850. A catalogue* (1924).

T. CHUBB, *The printed maps in the atlases of Great Britain and Ireland, 1579–1880. A bibliography* (1927).

E. HEAWOOD, *English county maps in the collection of the Royal Geographical Society* (1932). Facsimiles, with an introduction.

E. G. R. TAYLOR, *Tudor geography, 1485–1583* (1930).

E. G. R. TAYLOR, *Late Tudor and early Stuart geography, 1583–1650* (1934).

E. LYNAM, *British maps and map-makers* (1944).

E. LYNAM, 'English maps and map-makers of the 16th century', in *Geographical Journal*, cxvi (1950).

H. WHITAKER, *The Harold Whitaker Collection of county atlases, road-books & maps presented to the University of Leeds. A catalogue* (1947).

F. J. NORTH, *The map of Wales before 1600 A.D.* (1935).

F. J. NORTH, 'Humphrey Lhuyd's maps of England and of Wales', in *Archaeologia Cambrensis* (1937).

H. R. G. INGLIS (and others), *The early maps of Scotland* (2nd ed., 1936).

AMERICA

H. HARRISSE, *The discovery of North America . . . with an essay on the early cartography of the New World* (1892).

P. L. PHILLIPS, *A list of maps of America in the Library of Congress* (1901).

W. LOWERY, *A descriptive list of maps of the Spanish possessions within the present limits of the United States, 1502–1820* (1912).

I. N. PHELPS STOKES, *The iconography of Manhattan Island* (1915–28).

H. R. WAGNER, *The cartography of the northwest coast of America to the year 1800* (1937).

H. HARRISSE, *Notes pour servir à l'histoire, à la bibliographie et à la cartographie de la Nouvelle France, 1545–1700* (1872).

G. MARCEL, *Cartographie de la Nouvelle France* (1885).

PACIFIC OCEAN

L. WROTH, 'The early cartography of the Pacific', in *Papers of the Bibliographical Society of America*, xxxviii (1944).

Technique and history of engraving

Here is given a small selection of (*a*) general works, (*b*) general dictionaries of engravers, and (*c*) dictionaries of engravers of different countries. Of the third class, which is numerous and valuable for the study of early maps, only a few specimens are noted here. Reference should also be made to works on national biography for various countries, e.g. the *Dictionary of national biography*, *Les Belges illustres*, *Nieuw Nederlandsch woordenboek*, *Allgemeine deutsche Biographie*, etc.; and to works on the printing-trade.

A. M. HIND, *A history of engraving and etching* (3rd ed., 1923). With classified indexes of engravers and their work, and full bibliography.

BRITISH MUSEUM, *A guide to the processes and schools of engraving* (1923).

G. K. NAGLER, *Allgemeines Künstler-Lexikon* (1835–52).

U. THIEME and F. BECKER, *Allgemeines Lexikon der bildenden Künstler* (1907–47). Useful, like Nagler, especially for minor engravers.

SIR S. COLVIN, *Early engraving and engravers in England, 1545–1695* (1905).

A. M. HIND, *Engraving in England in the sixteenth and seventeenth centuries* (in preparation).

HORACE WALPOLE, *A catalogue of engravers* (1763).

A. M. HIND, *Early Italian engraving* (1938–48).

A. VON WURZBACH, *Niederländisches Künstlerlexikon* (1886).

J. G. WALLER, *Biographisch woordenboek van Noord-Nederlandsche graveurs* (1938).

Ornament and lettering

Of the extensive literature on these subjects, the following works are selected as directly useful in connection with early maps:

E. LYNAM, 'Period ornament, writing, and symbols on maps, 1250–1800', in *Geographical Magazine*, xviii (1945–6).

P. JESSEN, *Der Ornamentstich* (1920).

P. JESSEN, *Meister der Schreibkunst* (1923).

SIR A. HEAL, *The English writing-masters and their copy-books, 1570–1800* (1931).

A. FAIRBANK, *A book of scripts* (1949).

The book- and print-trades

The production and distribution of printed maps is an offshoot of these trades, and much information on early map-makers may be found in such reference books as those noted below. The book- and print-trades of the Netherlands are especially well-documented.

M. PLANT, *The English book trade* (1939).

BIBLIOGRAPHICAL SOCIETY, *A dictionary of printers and booksellers in England, Scotland and Ireland, 1557–1640*, by R. B. McKerrow (1910); *1641–1667*, by H. R. Plomer (1907); *1668–1725*, by H. R. Plomer (1922); *1726–1775*, by H. R. Plomer, G. H. Bushnell and E. R. McC. Dix (1932).

SIR A. HEAL, *The signboards of old London shops* (1947).

A. M. LEDEBOER, *De boekdrukkers, boekverkoopers, en uitgevers in Noord-Nederland* (1872).

E. W. MOES, *De Amsterdamsche boekdrukkers en uitgevers in de 16e eeuw* (1896–1915).

M. M. KLEERKOOPER and W. P. VAN STOCKUM, *De boekhandel te Amsterdam in de 17de eeuw* (1914–16).

F. KAPP, *Geschichte des deutschen Buchhandels* (1886).

Watermarks

C. M. BRIQUET, *Les filigranes* (1907). A *corpus* of watermarks before 1600.

E. HEAWOOD, *Watermarks, mainly of the 17th and 18th centuries* (1950). Continuing Briquet's work from 1600. Many of the examples were taken from maps. Reference should also be made to Heawood's articles on the subject in the *Geographical Journal* (1924, 1927) and in *The Library* (1928–31, 1948–9).

W. A. CHURCHILL, *Watermarks in paper in Holland, England, France, etc., in the XVII and XVIII centuries* (1935).

L. LE CLERT, *Le Papier* (1926). Mainly on French marks, especially those of Troyes papermakers.

G. H. BEANS, *Some sixteenth-century watermarks found in maps prevalent in the IATO atlases* (1938). On the marks of Italian maps.

I. Ptolemy

(Plates 1, 2)

THE GEOGRAPHICAL RENAISSANCE of the 15th century in Western Europe was introduced by the discovery and diffusion of Claudius Ptolemy's *Geographia*, a Greek manual on the construction and drawing of maps written at Alexandria about A.D. 160. Little is known of the fate of the book for a thousand years after Ptolemy's time. The earliest surviving Greek manuscripts, written between the 12th and 14th centuries, were brought to Italy by fugitive scholars on the collapse of the Byzantine Empire before A.D. 1400. The eight books into which the manuscripts were divided contained general instructions for map-making, tables of towns and physical features with their co-ordinates of latitude and longitude, and (in Book VIII) 26 maps of countries[1] with descriptive text; there was also a world-map signed by its maker Agathodaimon, whose date is not known.

The further stages by which the *Geographia* was made known to Western Europe were its Latin translation completed in 1409, the redrawing of the maps in Italy from about 1460, the first printing of the Latin text (in 1475) and of the maps (in 1477), and the addition of 'modern' maps to the Ptolemaic atlas, both in manuscripts and subsequent printed editions. From the maps redrawn by Donnus Nicolaus Germanus ('Master Nicholas the German'),[2] at Florence, and from other manuscript revisions, were printed the maps of the earliest editions: in those of Bologna 1477, Rome 1478, and Florence 1482 from copper plates, in that of Ulm 1482 from wood-blocks.

How much of Ptolemy's own work survived in the *Geographia*, in the form by which it became known to the West, is uncertain and hotly disputed by scholars.[3] In the history of Renaissance geography this question is less interesting than the acceptance of the *Geographia* as a genuine relic of classical science by humanists and cosmographers of the 15th century, to whom age spoke with authority. The impetus and direction which the treatise of 'Ptolemy' gave to geographical ideas and enterprise sprang not only from its supposed antiquity. Its mathematical approach to cartography was congenial to the experimental mind of Renaissance Italy, especially Florence; above all, its maps presented a systematic picture of the whole known world, drawn by a uniform method. The *Geographia* was the first world atlas. It coloured geographical thought until the end of the 16th century, and thirty-one Latin or Italian editions with maps were printed before 1600.

The expansion of the Ptolemaic world by the discovery of America and of the sea route to India did not destroy the *Geographia*'s credit among geographers. They grafted their new knowledge on to the stock of Ptolemy; and the hemispheric division of the globe, into the 'old world' of Ptolemy and the 'new world' to the west, dates from the early 16th century.[4] To the nucleus of 27 ancient maps, much revised, were added modern maps (increasing from four in the Florence edition of 1482 to thirty-seven in the Venice edition of 1561).

[1] Ten of Europe, four of Africa, twelve of Asia; these are known as the 'A-group'. Some manuscripts have, instead, 64 smaller regional maps (the 'B-group') scattered through the text of Books II–VII; these maps were never printed.

[2] They were reduced to the smaller size suitable for engraving and drawn on different projections; Nicolaus added a scale and inserted boundaries, shown by a dotted, or 'pricked', line.

[3] J. Fischer held that the 26 'country maps' of the A-group were derived from those drawn by Ptolemy to illustrate his text; L. Bagrow believes the text of the manuscripts to have been compiled (partly from Ptolemy's own works) by 'a Byzantine scholar, unknown to us, of the 10th–11th century', and the 26 maps to have been drawn from it by a Greek monk, Maximos Planudes, about 1300.

[4] Waldseemüller's two-fold sources are indicated in the title of his great world map of 1507: 'Universalis Cosmographia secundum Ptolomaei traditionem et Americi Vespucii aliorumque lustrationes' – according to the tradition of Ptolemy and the voyages of Amerigo Vespucci and others.

All were drawn and engraved in the manner of their day, and the successive editions of Ptolemy illustrate the development of cartographic technique.

The growth of the 'modern' section in these editions culminated naturally in the atlas of wholly modern maps, the idea of which, conceived by Italian map-publishers, was triumphantly realised by Ortelius in 1570. Although Mercator's great edition of Ptolemy (1578) was still to come,[1] the modern atlas gradually drove the Ptolemaic maps from the field; but cartographers continued to pay tribute to Ptolemy explicitly or by imitation. An Italian publisher, making a collection of maps for a customer, would arrange them 'secondo l'ordine di Tolomeo' – in Ptolemy's order; and this sequence was followed not only by Ortelius and Mercator but even in the Dutch atlases of the next century. Ortelius, wishing to compliment Mercator, called him 'the Ptolemy of our day'; in 1589 Thomas Blundeville wrote a *Briefe Description of Universal Maps and Cards . . . and also the use of Ptolemy his Tables*; and the first atlas devoted wholly to America, that by C. Wytfliet (1597), was styled *Descriptionis Ptolemaicae augmentum* – a supplement to Ptolemy.

Complete lists of the editions of Ptolemy may be found in works noted in the Bibliography to this chapter; the following list epitomises the maps of editions published before 1600:

1477, *Bologna*	Line-engraved.
1478, *Rome*	Line-engraved. Reprinted 1490, Rome; with added maps 1507, Rome; 1508, Rome.
1482, *Florence*	Line-engraved. Italian text.
1482, *Ulm*	Woodcut. Reprinted 1486, Ulm.
1511, *Venice*	Woodcut.
1513, *Strassburg*	Woodcut. Edited by Martin Waldseemüller, with 20 modern maps. Reprinted 1520, Strassburg.
1522, *Strassburg*	Woodcut. Edited by Laurent Fries. Reprinted 1525, Strassburg; 1535, Lyons; 1541, Vienne.
1540, *Basle*	Woodcut. Edited by Sebastian Münster. Reprinted 1542, 1545, 1552, all at Basle.
1548, *Venice*	Line-engraved, by Jacopo Gastaldi. Italian text.
1561, *Venice*	Line-engraved. Italian text. Reprinted 1562, 1564, 1574, 1598–9, all at Venice.
1578, *Cologne*	Line-engraved, by Mercator. Reprinted 1584, Cologne; 1602, Düsseldorf; 1605, Amsterdam; 1695; 1698; 1704; 1730.
1596, *Venice*	Line-engraved. Edited by G. A. Magini. Reprinted 1597–8, Venice; 1597, Cologne; 1608, Cologne; 1617, Arnhem; 1621, Padua.

BIBLIOGRAPHY

The literature on Ptolemy is vast, and only a few more important or useful works can be noted here.

The English translation of the *Geographia* by E. L. STEVENSON (1932) has an introduction by J. FISCHER containing his views on the transmission of the text and maps; these are set out more fully in FISCHER's introduction (in German) to his facsimile edition of an early Vatican MS. (1932). They are disputed by L. BAGROW, *The Origin of Ptolemy's Geographia* (1946), which also summarises earlier studies. An important work on the MSS. is: O. CUNTZ, *Die Geographie des Ptolemäus* (1923).

Older lists of printed editions are: WILBERFORCE EAMES, *List of editions of Ptolemy's Geography, 1475–1730* (1886); J. WINSOR, *Bibliography of Ptolemy's Geography* (1888); and H. N. STEVENS, *Ptolemy's*

---

[1] But this was in fact a historical atlas, for it reproduced only the ancient maps.

I. PTOLEMY

Geography (1908). R. V. TOOLEY, *Maps and map-makers* (1949), pp. 6–8, gives a convenient list based on STEVENS. A definitive bibliography, by W. H. STAHL, is announced by the New York Public Library.

A full account of early editions is in A. E. NORDENSKIÖLD, *Facsimile Atlas* (1889), which reproduces all the maps of the 1490 edition. The Italian editions of the 15th century are described by A. M. HIND, *Early Italian engraving* (1938), vol. I, pp. 290–298; by E. LYNAM, *The first engraved atlas of the world: the Cosmographia of C. Ptolemaeus, Bologna 1477* (1941); and by A. CODAZZI, *Le edizioni quattrocenteschi e cinquecenteschi della 'Geografia' di Tolomeo* (1950).

Studies of Ptolemy as a geographer will be found in works on Greek geography, e.g. by E. H. BUNBURY (1879), H. F. TOZER (new edition 1935), E. H. WARMINGTON (1934). There is an acute examination of the cartographic problems in T. G. RYLANDS, *The Geography of Ptolemy elucidated* (1893).

NOTES ON THE ILLUSTRATIONS

Plate 1   Western Germany, from the 'Quarta Tabula Europae' in Ptolemy's *Geographia* printed at Rome by Arnold Buckinck in 1478. Line-engraving. Original size. The engravers of Buckinck's maps had been trained by his predecessor Conrad Sweynheym from about 1474, but the book was not ready until a year after the first edition of Ptolemy with maps, that of Bologna in 1477. The style of engraving, although more sophisticated than that of the Bologna maps, is stiff and has an archaic dignity. All lettering is in roman capitals of different sizes, and decoration is absent. Mountains are conical and shaded on the east; three types of forest are distinguished; rivers rise in ponds and issue in gushing estuaries. Towns are represented by circles.

Plate 2   World map, in Ptolemy's *Geographia* edited by Nicolaus Germanus and printed by Lienhart Holle at Ulm in 1482. Woodcut. Size of original 16" × 22". This is the earliest map signed by an engraver (Johann Schnitzer of Armsheim). It shows the Ptolemaic world covering 180° of longitude and 88° of latitude, with a landlocked Indian Ocean, and is drawn on Nicolaus' spherical projection. Degrees are marked in the right-hand and top and bottom margins of the map; and at the left are indicated Ptolemy's parallels giving the length (in hours) of the longest day at different latitudes. The only attempts at decoration are the twelve wind faces in the border, with their Greek names enclosed in scrolls. Roman capitals and a clear carolingian minuscule are used for names. Mountain ranges are outlined in plan (a convention introduced by Nicolaus).

II. Woodcut Maps

(Plates 3–10)

The maps in the Italian editions of Ptolemy of the 15th century were printed from copper plates, but the superior flexibility and 'looseness' of this technique had not yet been appreciated by cartographers. In the cities of South Germany and the Rhineland, and in Venice – which had close connections with Germany – flourishing schools of wood-engravers were at work, and the woodcut was the recognised medium for book-illustration and design. This was the process by which nearly all important maps before the middle of the 16th century were printed. The convenience of a relief technique commended it for the printing of maps with letterpress,[1] but it was generally used also for sheet-maps whether from single blocks or (like the wall-maps of Waldseemüller and Caspar Vopel) from as many as twelve blocks; the woodcut sheet maps popular in Central Europe at this period are to-day extremely rare.

Although in the first half of the 16th century Spain and Portugal retained the initiative in discovery, it was from the Rhineland towns of Strassburg and (a generation later) Basle that the new geography was diffused and popularised in pamphlets, travel collections and maps. Geographers of Lorraine, whose works were printed at Strassburg, corrected and supplemented Ptolemy with material from Portuguese charts and Italian reports of the great discoveries, and to them is due the introduction of the name 'America'.[2] The cartographic masterpieces of this school, all printed from wood-blocks, are Martin Waldseemüller's edition of Ptolemy (1513) and his large wall-maps – the world map of 1507, a road map of Europe now lost (1511), and a world chart (1516).

But the real centres of geographical activity lay farther east, in Bavaria and Franconia. The Imperial cities of Nuremberg and Augsburg lay at the meeting-point of European trade and communications; the great commercial houses of Fugger and Welser had correspondents in all countries; merchant patrons like Konrad Peutinger and Willibald Pirckheimer fostered geographical studies; and, especially in Nuremberg, mathematical and astronomical science, with the auxiliary craft of instrument-making, had flourished since the early 15th century. These cities nourished vigorous printing industries and were the home of many famous woodcut artists, notably Albrecht Dürer, Hans Burgkmair and Hans Holbein.[3] To the close alliance between the crafts of book-printing, map-reproduction and wood-engraving[4] may be traced both the technical accomplishment of German woodcut maps in the middle decades of the 16th century and the experiment of combining metal types with the wood-block.[5]

The theoretical bent of German geographers lay in the direction of mathematical cartography; their practical interest, in 'chorography' or descriptive regional geography. From the second quarter of the century, the detailed mapping of provinces and regions was carried on in other countries (especially Italy and Flanders), but in none more actively than in Germany. Road maps of the environs of Nuremberg were printed before 1500; Waldsee-

---

[1] See Introduction, p. 2.

[2] The first printed map to show the new lands in the west is Contarini's world map of 1506; the first to give the name America (but to the southern part of the continent only) is Waldseemüller's world map of 1507; the first to apply it to both parts of the continent is Mercator's world map of 1538.

[3] The maps and views in the Nuremberg Chronicle (1493) were cut by Dürer's master, Michael Wohlgemut, and another engraver.

[4] The cartographer Peter Apian set up a printing press at Ingolstadt; and a contemporary geographer, Johann Honter, introduced printing in Transylvania.

[5] See Introduction, pp. 3, 14.

müller's edition of Ptolemy had included three regional maps of the Rhineland countries; and in 1528 Sebastian Münster, the 'German Strabo', called on German geographers[1] to survey their home provinces and to send him their maps, 'so that all Germany with its villages, towns, trades, etc. may be seen as in a mirror'. Many of the maps which he received in reply to his appeal were printed by Münster, with acknowledgments, in his edition of Ptolemy (1540) and in his *Cosmographia* (1545); and Münster may be said to have devised the atlas of composite authorship, of the type later made familiar by Italian map-collections and by the *Theatrum* of Ortelius.

The mapping of smaller areas demanded a more comprehensive vocabulary of conventional signs, which appear in ingenious variety, as in Philipp Apian's map of Bavaria (Pl. 10b). The Nuremberg geographers, living at the great commercial crossroads of South Germany, were the first to produce printed road maps (Pl. 3b); and German cartographers, then (as since) sensitive to frontiers, led the way in delineating political and administrative boundaries on maps. The 'national', or nationalist, character of German map-making is betrayed no less in the persistent use of gothic lettering, both in engraved maps and in letterpress printing.

The most important work by German cartographers of this period was done before 1550, but its influence was extended by many later reprints. New editions of the two most popular geography books of the century, the Cosmographies of Peter Apian and Sebastian Münster,[2] continued to appear, with maps and town plans from the original blocks, until the beginning of the 17th century.

BIBLIOGRAPHY

L. GALLOIS, *Les géographes allemands de la Renaissance* (1890).

E. LEHMANN, *Alte deutsche Landkarten* (1935).

H. PRAESENT, *Beiträge zur deutschen Kartographie* (1921).

A. HERRMANN, *Die ältesten Karten Deutschlands* (1940).

H. KRÜGER, 'Erhard Etzlaub and his "Romweg" map', in *Imago Mundi*, VIII (1951).

W. LANG, 'The Augsburg travel guide of 1563 and the Erlinger road map of 1524', in *Imago Mundi*, VII (1950).

J. FISCHER and F. R. VON WIESER, *Die älteste Karte mit dem Namen America aus dem Jahre 1507 und die Carta Marina aus dem Jahre 1517 des M. Waldseemüller* (1903).

S. GÜNTHER, *Peter und Philipp Apian* (1882).

O. HUPP, *Philipp Apian's Bayerische Landtafeln und Peter Weiner's Chorographia Bavariae* (1910).

V. HANTZSCH, *Sebastian Münster* (1898).

W. HORN, 'Sebastian Münster's map of Prussia and the variants of it', in *Imago Mundi*, VII (1950).

L. WEISZ, *Die Schweiz auf alten Karten* (1945).

T. ISCHL, *Die ältesten Karten der Eidgenossenschaft* (1945).

NOTES ON THE ILLUSTRATIONS

Plate 3a   The 'Tabula Terre Nove', in Ptolemy's *Geographia* edited by Waldseemüller and printed at Strassburg in 1513 and 1520. Woodcut. Size of original $14\frac{1}{2}$" × $17\frac{1}{2}$". The first map

---

[1] In a pamphlet describing an instrument for plane-table survey. A year later Münster settled at Basle.

[2] Apian's *Cosmographicus liber* was published at Landshut, in Bavaria, in 1524; the enlarged edition edited by the Flemish geographer Gemma Frisius, with the title *Cosmographia*, first appeared in 1533 and was translated into several languages. Münster's *Cosmographia*, printed in 1545, was revised and expanded in the edition of 1550, which contained many new maps and town-plans (Pl. 9, 10a). The emphasis in Apian's work was on astronomy and mathematical geography, in Münster's on topography and history.

devoted entirely to the New World in an edition of Ptolemy; an inscription in South America refers to its discovery by Columbus. Lettering is in a cursive book hand and roman capitals; the influence of charts is seen in the placing of coastal names at right angles to the shore-line. There is a scale of Italian miles (10 = one division); and, as in all the 'modern' maps added to Ptolemy by Waldseemüller, latitudes are marked in the margin but not longitudes. The zig-zag sea shading recalls a device used much later by Flemish engravers. There is no other decoration.

Plate 3b   Road-map of the environs of Nuremberg, unsigned and undated; early 16th century. Woodcut. Size of original 7½″ × 4½″. Reproduced from the copy in the British Museum. Maps of this type were made at Nuremberg from 1492 by the compass-maker Erhard Etzlaub. Below is a smaller map of the environs of Bamberg. Roads are dotted lines; names are in a squat gothic letter; four wind-faces are the only decoration. The scales are in German miles.

Plate 4   Southern Asia ('Indiae Tabula Moderna'), in Ptolemy's *Geographia* edited by Laurent Fries (Strassburg 1522 and 1525) and by Michael Servet (Lyons 1535, Vienne 1541). Woodcut. Size of original 11½″ × 17½″. A reduction of the 'modern' map of Waldseemüller's edition. Scale in German miles; divisions of latitude but not of longitude. The engraving and lettering resemble those of the first Strassburg edition (Pl. 3a). The vignettes illustrate stories from medieval lore.

Plate 5   North Africa, in Ptolemy's *Geographia* edited by Sebastian Münster (Basle 1540, 1545, 1550, 1552). Woodcut, with place-names printed from metal type. Size of original 10″ × 13½″. The Ptolemaic map ('Secunda Tabula Africae'), with a lively picture of St Paul's shipwreck added. Mountains are overlapping cones, shaded on the west.

Plate 6   England, in Münster's Ptolemy. Woodcut, with place-names from metal type. Size of original 10″ × 13½″. The first printed modern map of England; Münster corrects Ptolemy's erroneous plotting of Scotland on an EW axis. East is at the top of the map. The pictorial town-symbols are perhaps copied from Münster's MS. original. With the national flags of England and Scotland.

Plate 7   The New World, in Münster's Ptolemy. Woodcut, with place-names from metal type. Size of original 10″ × 13½″. Another of Münster's 'modern' maps. The geography of the West coast of America ('Catigara', 'Zipangu', the 7,448 islands in the China Sea) is borrowed from Marco Polo's account of eastern Asia; so are the cannibals, first marked in Brazil by Laurent Fries (1522). With flags of Portugal, off the African coast, and Spain, in the West Indies.

Plate 8   World-map, on a heart-shaped projection, in Peter Apian's *Cosmographia* edited by Gemma Frisius (Antwerp 1545, and later editions). Woodcut. Size of original 7½″ × 10½″. The lettering is engraved in an irregular cursive and roman capitals. The decoration includes ships and monsters on the map; the signs of the zodiac and Ptolemy's 'climates' in the inner border; and an elaborate arrangement of wind-faces in solid-looking clouds, surmounted by Mars and Neptune.

Plate 9   Bird's-eye view of Paris, in Münster's *Cosmographia* (Basle 1550, and later editions to 1628). Woodcut, with names printed from metal type. Size of original 6½″ × 10″. The 1550 edition of Münster's book contained over 60 town-plans or views. Top left is the 'key', framed in acanthus leaves, and top right a shield of fleurs-de-lis. Two gallows are conspicuous among the perspective details. Fences indicate enclosed land outside the city.

Plate 10a View of Edinburgh, in the same work. Woodcut, with lettering from metal type. Size of original 4″ × 7.″ Topographically worthless, but typical of the almost symbolic character of such early representations of towns.

II. WOODCUT MAPS

Plate 10b Detail from Philipp Apian's *Bairische Landtaflen XXIIII* (Ingolstadt 1568), plate 13. Woodcut, with names from metal type. Original size. The table gives conventional signs for Imperial cities, bishoprics, monasteries, towns, markets, castles, villages, glass-works, salt-pans, mines, medicinal waters (and boundaries, off). Roads are marked by dotted lines. Within the decorative borders, the work of the wood-engraver Jost Amman of Zurich, the distances of important towns (Marsilia 94, Lyon 65) are indicated as in modern maps; the inner margin is graduated in miles, and each five-mile division is lettered for reference. The grid, with numbered rectangles, has been added in ink by a later owner of the map.

III. Italian Maps
The Revival of Line-Engraving

(Plates 11, 12, 42)

The characteristic fruit of German descriptive geography was Münster's *Cosmographia*, a massive volume of text interspersed with woodcut maps and views of towns and many other vignettes and pictures. In Italy, where the making of manuscript maps and charts was still a flourishing industry, a more graphic tradition prevailed, and the popular form for printed maps was the separate sheet rather than the book-illustration. Most maps printed in Italy, as elsewhere, before the middle of the 16th century were woodcuts. The stock of Rosselli's shop at Florence in 1527[1] included many wood-blocks; and in Venice, the Mediterranean outlet for trade from Central Europe, wood-engravers practised their craft in active association with the schools of South Germany. The first Venice edition of Ptolemy (1511) had woodcut maps, with legends printed from metal types; and the sheet maps of the Venetian printer-cartographers G. A. Vavassore and Matheo Pagano,[2] all published before 1562, were cut in wood.

In Italy, however, the craft of engraving on copper and the printseller's trade had long been established independently of the book industry, whose purposes were better served by wood-engraving. From the engraving of antiquities and topographical subjects to that of maps was a short step; and the greater control of his line enjoyed by the cartographer working on copper instead of wood was exploited by Italian map-engravers from about 1540. The first edition of Ptolemy printed in Italy after 1511, that of Venice 1548, with maps engraved by Jacopo Gastaldi,[3] marks the turn of the tide in favour of copper. Of the eighteen Ptolemaic atlases published before this date, twelve had maps printed from wood-blocks, but only one of the thirteen editions from 1548 to 1600 had woodcut maps. But the staple of the Italian map-trade was the line-engraved sheet maps with which it captured the European market.

The centres of this trade were Rome and Venice, and the map workshops of these cities were controlled by masters who combined the activities of cartographer, engraver, printer, publisher, and mapseller.[4] The most active of these masters were:

Rome   Antonio Lafreri, a native of Besançon, who published his first print at Rome in 1544 and was in business as a map- and print-seller from 1553–63 in partnership with Antonio Salamanca, and from 1563 till his death in 1577 alone.

Michele Tramezini, active 1539–82.

Claudio Duchetti, Lafreri's successor, who died in 1585.

Venice   G. F. Camocio, active 1558–75.

Paolo Forlani, active 1560–74.

Donato and Ferrando Bertelli, active 1559–74.

Their output was copious and (from the geographer's point of view) uneven, for its character was determined by the need to supply an expanding demand both in Italy and abroad. The stock of maps for sale in a printshop was replenished not only by impressions from plates engraved in the shop; both impressions and plates were purchased from other publishers. While the stock included original maps of Italian provinces and towns, the

---

[1] See Introduction, p. 5.

[2] See L. Bagrow, *G. A. Vavassore: a descriptive list of his maps* (1939), and *Matheo Pagano: a descriptive list of his maps* (1940).

[3] After those of Münster.   [4] See Introduction, pp. 5–6.

plates representing other countries were generally copied or adapted from the maps of foreign cartographers. The engraving technique found (with personal variations) in all this work is distinguished by precision of line, by finely drawn but restrained decoration, and by roman and italic lettering of great clarity and often beauty. Gastaldi stands out among his contemporaries for geographical originality, for fertility, and for his technical brilliance as cartographic draughtsman and engraver.

To the Italian mapsellers, working to orders from their customers, is due the prototype of the modern atlas. This was not a true atlas in our sense, made up of impressions from plates uniform in size and design. It was simply a set of maps, covering the world, put together from the mapseller's stock – mainly impressions from his own plates but completed (if necessary) from those of other firms. There was, however, some system in the compilation of such atlases, between 60 and 70 copies of which have survived. Maps of various sizes were made up to the dimensions of the volume, by mounting on blank paper; and when the added margins have the same watermark throughout, the original date and place at which a volume was assembled can be inferred.[1] The maps in these collections were arranged in a standard order, that of Ptolemy; and in some Roman collections a title-page, engraved about 1570, is found: 'Tavole moderne di Geografia de la maggior parte del mondo di diversi autori raccolte et messe secondo l'ordine di Tolomeo . . . stampate in rame . . . in Roma.' The name 'Lafreri atlas'[2] was prompted by the Roman imprint of this title and by the similarity between Lafreri's list of about 1573[3] and the contents of such collections; but Venetian atlases put together by Camocio, Forlani or Bertelli are more common than those of the Roman dealers. The maps in these collections are dated from 1546 to 1583, with a few stragglers earlier and later; but dates between 1560 and 1570 are most common.

The most important contribution to Italian regional cartography in the middle of the century was that of Gastaldi, and the first regional atlas of Italy, G. A. Magini's *Italia*, although begun before 1600, was published only in 1620 (Pl. 42).

BIBLIOGRAPHY

G. Uzielli and P. Amat di San Filippo, *Studi . . . sulla storia della geografia in Italia* (1882).

G. Marinelli, *Saggio di cartografia italiana* (1893).

G. Marinelli, *Saggio di cartografia della regione veneta* (1881).

R. Almagià, *Monumenta Italiae cartographica* (1929).

R. Almagià, *L'Italia di G. A. Magini* (1922).

R. Almagià, *Monumenta cartographica Vaticana* (1944–49, etc.).

A. E. Nordenskiöld, *Facsimile Atlas* (1889).

F. C. Wieder, *Nederlandsche historisch-geographische documenten in Spanje* (1915).

R. V. Tooley, 'Maps in Italian atlases of the sixteenth century', in *Imago Mundi*, III (1939).

S. Grande, *Notizie sulla vita e sulle opere di Giacomo Gastaldi* (1902).

NOTES ON THE ILLUSTRATIONS

Plate 11   Detail (the Gulf of Venice) from Jacopo Gastaldi's map of S.E. Europe, 'La discrittione della Transiluania . . .', published by Paolo Forlani, Venice, 1566. Original size. Line-engraving. The cartographic design and decoration are severe, the lettering a neat italic. Hills are

---

[1] See E. Heawood, 'An undescribed Lafreri atlas and contemporary Venetian collections', in *Geographical Journal*, lxxiii (1929), pp. 359–369.

[2] Suggested by Nordenskiöld. Mr George H. Beans proposes the term 'I A T O' – Italian atlases assembled to order. The contents of known copies of the atlas have been analysed by Tooley (1939).

[3] See Introduction, p. 6. The map-section in Lafreri's list has a sub-title whose wording is almost identical with that of the title-page referred to above.

drawn in profile and unshaded; the sea is stippled, with coastal shading; towns are drawn in perspective.

Plate 12   Detail (Abyssinia) from 'Africae Tabula VIIII', in the *Geografia* of Livio Sanuto (Venice
 1588). Original size. Sanuto's finely engraved maps represent 16th-century Italian line-
work on copper in its maturity. Hills are shaded or hatched on the east slope; towns represented by
a circle, with towers added in profile to indicate their importance. The pictorial detail includes the
tents of the Emperor and his army (as in medieval maps), and the 'royal mountain' in which the sons
of the Emperor live.

Plate 42   Detail of 'Territorio di Bergamo', in the *Italia* of G. A. Magini edited by his son Fabio
 (Bologna 1620). Original size. Line-engraving. The line is heavier, the shading coarser,
and the strapwork ornament imitates Flemish work. Towns are depicted by circles, the larger ones
drawn in perspective. Many maps in the *Italia* were engraved by Benjamin Wright, a Londoner who
worked abroad.

IV. Map-Engravers of the Netherlands 16th Century

(Plates 13–30)

The Italian maps did not satisfy the more scientific geographers of the Low Countries. The 'rule of truth', wrote Mercator to Ortelius, was neglected in many maps, and he added that those from Italy were 'specially bad in this respect'. Mercator himself is pre-eminent as a cartographer in whom geographical scholarship was allied to technical ability as a map-draughtsman and engraver. A map-engraver of the next generation, Jodocus Hondius, singled out this combination of talents in his eulogy of Mercator, who (he wrote) 'to his knowledge of geography and chronology added a quality exceedingly rare among scholars, a skill in drawing, engraving, and elegant illuminating'; and another panegyrist described Mercator as 'ingenio dexter, dexter et ipse manu' – gifted both in mind and hand.

At Louvain, from about 1535 until he moved to Duisburg in 1552, Mercator won a reputation as a maker of mathematical and astronomical instruments, working first for Gemma Frisius and later independently. To this period belong his large globes (1541–51) and the splendid 'cosmos' which he constructed for the Emperor Charles V, formed of an outer celestial globe of glass with a wooden terrestrial globe set at its centre. Mercator's first map, published in 1537, was engraved on copper, and this technique was doubtless commended to him both by his experience in metal-working and by his perception of the greater control and precision of line (in comparison with wood-engraving) which it gave to the cartographer. So too the italic script, on which he published a manual in 1540,[1] was plainly that which enabled the map-maker to write and engrave names most clearly, to place them correctly, and to work them harmoniously into his design; for this is a script which (as an English writing-master[2] claimed) can be written 'with singular command of the hand'. The lettering on Mercator's maps invariably serves his geographical purpose and satisfies the standards of freedom and discipline required in cartography; his treatise eschews pointless flourishes and ornament, and a similar sobriety is found in the decoration of his maps (Pl. 13).

Mercator's geographical achievement has been the subject of many studies[3] and will not be discussed here. Unlike many of his contemporaries, he was an original, not a reproductive, engraver, and nearly all his maps were both drawn and engraved by him. (An exception is the great map of the British Isles which he engraved in 1564 from a draft sent to him by an unidentified 'English friend'.) This indeed partly explains his comparatively small output; in a letter of 1583 he complained that the progress of his Atlas was delayed by shortage of engravers, all the work being done by himself and two grandsons.[4]

The reputation enjoyed by Mercator in his day is indicated not only by contemporary tributes but (more explicitly) by the diffusion of his works. The demand for his large globes continued till the end of the century, and Plantin's ledgers record the sale (between 1558 and 1576) of no fewer than 868 copies of his wall map of Europe, published in 1554 and revised in 1572. It was inevitable that, in the drawing, lettering and engraving of maps, Mercator's manner should be copied and elaborated by other craftsmen of the Netherlands

---

[1] *Literarum Latinarum, quas Italicas, cursoriasque vocant, scribendarum ratio* (Antwerp 1540). It is curious that this treatise, like the Italian writing-books which preceded it, was printed from wood-blocks.

[2] Martin Billingsley (1618).   [3] See the Bibliography, p. 48.

[4] Here is sufficient cause for the slowness of Mercator's work on the Atlas and his failure to complete it. The once popular tradition, originating in the 17th century, that he postponed publication to avoid competition with his friend Ortelius, is now discredited.

and neighbouring countries. These engravers found their opportunity in the great atlases, uniform in presentation but eclectic in their sources, for which the *Theatrum orbis terrarum* of Ortelius set the fashion.

The *Theatrum*, published at Antwerp in 1570, may be considered the first modern atlas, compiled on principles laid down by its editor and not to satisfy the fancy of a customer.[1] Yet its origin recalls that of the Italian atlases. In the early 1560's Ortelius, then in business as an illuminator and seller of maps, was requested by the merchant adventurer Egidius Hooftman to put together for him a collection of maps of Europe convenient to handle ('not larger than a sheet of paper'). This volume of 38 maps, the prototype of the famous atlas, still existed, somewhat battered, in 1604, but is now lost; it contained about 30 maps printed at Rome by Tramezini and seven or eight engraved in Belgium. Within ten years the first edition of the *Theatrum* had appeared, with 70 maps on 53 plates, almost all of which were engraved 'by the cunning hand of Frans Hogenberg' at Cologne. That it was designed as an atlas, and not a 'set of maps', is shown by Ortelius's refusal to put separate sheets on sale before the whole work was ready.

Ortelius was not an original cartographer,[2] but his respect for his sources is revealed not only in instructions to his agents to procure the best maps, but also in the 'Catalogue of authors' which he prefixed to each edition of the atlas. The list in the first edition contains the names of 87 cartographers, and this was extended in successive editions until in that of 1603 it numbered 183 names. As Bagrow remarks in his invaluable study of this catalogue, we owe it to Ortelius that a whole series of 16th-century cartographers have not remained altogether unknown.

The popularity of the *Theatrum* was immediate and continued until the beginning of the 17th century, when Hondius, the owner of Mercator's plates, conquered the market with his own atlas. To 'engravers, illuminators, and binders', as a contemporary records, Ortelius's enterprise brought prosperity, and until nearly 1600 the south Netherlands remained the centre of the map industry. Not only did the numerous and expanding editions of the *Theatrum* provide work for all kinds of craftsmen associated with the printing of maps and atlases; it also created a vogue for large cartographic projects. It is true that the finely engraved atlas of Gerard de Jode, the *Speculum orbis terrarum* published at Antwerp in 1578, was a commercial failure, stifled perhaps by the rivalry of Ortelius. Mercator's atlas, the first part of which was printed in 1585, had been conceived many years earlier as part of a great treatise on creation; its success was due to Mercator's own reputation, and (as we have seen) it was engraved by Mercator and his family. But other grandiose collections – the city atlas of Georg Braun and Frans Hogenberg published between 1572 and 1618, Waghenaer's sea-atlases of 1584 and 1592, Theodore de Bry's *America* (1590–1634) – provided contracts in plenty for the family workshops of Flemish engravers at home or in exile; and their output, both in sheet- and atlas-maps, was immense.

Many of these engravers worked abroad, where their activity made the Flemish manner in map-engraving the model for native craftsmen. The brothers Frans and Remigius Hogenberg were natives of Malines. Remigius settled in England, and was one of the 'drawers and cutters' maintained by Archbishop Parker at Lambeth; nine of Saxton's plates (1574–77) and John Hooker's plan of Exeter (1587) were engraved by him. Frans, after engraving the maps for the first edition of Ortelius's atlas, established himself as a type-cutter and founder[3]

---

[1] See L. Bagrow, *Abrahami Ortelii catalogus cartographorum*, pt. I (1928), p. II.

[2] Only five maps by him are known before 1570.

[3] This craft has not infrequently been associated with that of copper-plate engraving. Among other map-engravers who practised it may be mentioned Jodocus Hondius, in the 16th century, and Joseph Moxon, in the 17th.

at Cologne, where he set himself to remove the reproach of Mercator that the booksellers of Cologne were not interested in geographical publications. He continued to work for Ortelius, and the great city atlas, the *Civitates orbis terrarum*, edited by Georg Braun and engraved and sold by Hogenberg, was designed as a companion to the *Theatrum* and compiled by the same methods. The plates of towns in the Netherlands were from the plans of Jacob van Deventer, also an exile in Cologne; fifteen views[1] were supplied by the brilliant topographical artist Georg Hoefnagel; and correspondents in other countries were exhorted to send the 'portrait' of their native places to be engraved by Hogenberg. The representation of towns in his plates (Pl. 19–22) is picturesque rather than geometrical; they are usually drawn in bird's-eye view and set in romantic landscapes; in the foreground are figures of the inhabitants in local costume.[2] But, allowing for the engraver's licence, the collection of Braun and Hogenberg is a valuable source for 16th-century topography; like that of Ortelius, it preserved work which would otherwise have been lost and it began the vogue for 'town-books' which bore generous fruit in the next century.

Other prolific Dutch or Flemish engravers of this period were the brothers Jan and Lucas van Deutecum, working at Haarlem and Amsterdam, who engraved the maps in de Jode's *Speculum* (1578) and in Waghenaer's sea-atlases, the *Spieghel der zeevaert* (1584) and *Thresoor der zeevaert* (1592); the sons of Jan van Deutecum, Jan the younger and Baptista, the latter of whom with his father engraved the views in Jan Huyghen van Linschoten's *Itinerario* (1596); Ferdinand and Ambrosius Arsenius (Aertsen), the grandsons of Gemma Frisius, who, working at Cologne, engraved plates for Ortelius's atlas after the death of Hogenberg in 1591; the van Langeren family of Malines, Jacob Florensz. and his sons Arnold and Hendrik, who also engraved the maps in Linschoten's book (Pl. 28, 29); and Theodore de Bry, a native of Liège who set up a workshop with his sons at Frankfort. De Bry had visited London, where he engraved some of the charts (Pl. 24) in the English edition of Waghenaer's *Spieghel*, *The Mariners Mirrour* (1588); and here, with the help of Richard Hakluyt, he obtained the drawings of Virginia by John White and of Florida by Jacques Le Moyne from which he engraved the plates in the first two volumes of his collection of discoveries in the 'West and East India'.[3] The decoration in de Bry's maps is original in its gaiety and freedom (Pl. 24–26).

The three great atlases which dominated the last quarter of the 16th century suffered very different fates. The popularity of the *Theatrum* did not long survive Ortelius's death in 1598. The copper plates were sold by his widow to J. B. Vrients (who had also acquired those of de Jode), and the last edition was printed in 1612, when Vrients died; the plates remained in the possession of the Moret family, Plantin's successors, until 1704, but were not again printed.[4] Mercator's *Atlas*, painfully completed by his son Rumold in 1595, enjoyed a long career after its plates came in turn into the possession of Hondius, his successor Jan Jansson, and Jansson's heirs.[5] The *Civitates* of Braun and Hogenberg, the first three volumes of which were published between 1572 and Frans Hogenberg's death in 1591, were completed by three further volumes, the last of which appeared in 1618; these plates also passed into Jansson's stock and thence into that of Frederik de Wit, and impressions from them were published till the end of the 17th century.[6]

[1] Nine Spanish, four French, two English.   [2] See Introduction, p. 18.

[3] The *Collectiones Peregrinationum*, or 'Grands et Petits Voyages', begun by de Bry in 1590 and completed by M. Merian in 1634. The drawings by White are now in the British Museum.

[4] But an enlarged edition of the *Parergon* – the section of historical maps – was published in 1624, and with it (apparently) the *Theatrum* of 1612 was reissued.

[5] See below, Chapter VI.

[6] Jansson reprinted them in 1657, his heirs in 1682, and de Wit later still.

BIBLIOGRAPHY

H. E. WAUWERMANS, *Histoire de l'école cartographique belge et anversoise du XVIe siecle* (1895).

J. DENUCÉ, *Oudnederlandsche kaartmakers in betrekking met Plantijn* (1912).

F. C. WIEDER, *Monumenta cartographica* (1925–34).

S. J. FOCKEMA ANDREAE and B. VAN'T HOFF, *Geschiedenis der kartografie van Nederlanden* (1947).

J. KEUNING, 'Dutch cartography in the XVIth century', in *Imago Mundi*, IX (1952).

P. A. TIELE, *Nederlandsche bibliographie van land- en volkenkunde* (1884).

A. VON WURZBACH, *Niederländisches Künstlerlexikon* (1904–11).

F. VAN ORTROY, *Bio-bibliographie de Gemma Frisius . . . et de ses neveux les Arsenius* (1920).

J. VAN RAEMDONCK, *Gérard Mercator, sa vie et ses oeuvres* (1869).

H. AVERDUNK and J. MÜLLER-REINHARDT, *Gerhard Mercator und die Geographen unter seinen Nachkommen* (1914).

F. VAN ORTROY, *Bibliographie sommaire de l'oeuvre mercatorienne* (1920).

J. KEUNING, 'The history of an atlas: Mercator-Hondius', in *Imago Mundi*, IV (1947).

J. H. HESSELS, *Abrahami Ortelii . . . epistulae* (1887).

M. ROOSES, 'Ortelius et Plantin', in *Bulletin de la Soc. Géogr. d'Anvers*, v (1880).

L. BAGROW, *Abrahami Ortelii catalogus cartographorum* (1928–30).

F. VAN ORTROY, *Gérard de Jode et son oeuvre* (1914).

A. E. POPHAM, 'Georg Hoefnagel and the Civitates orbis terrarum', in *Maso Finiguerra*, i (1936).

F. BACHMANN, *Die alten Städtebilder* (1939).

D. GERNEZ, 'Lucas Janszoon Wagenaer', in *Mariner's Mirror*, xxiii (1937).

M. S. GIUSEPPI, 'The work of Theodore de Bry and his sons, engravers', in *Proceedings of the Huguenot Society of London*, xi (1915–17).

A. G. CAMUS, *Mémoire sur la collection des Grands et Petits Voyages* (1802).

EARL OF CRAWFORD AND BALCARRES, *Grands et Petits Voyages of De Bry* (1884).

Note: A list of the editions of Ortelius's *Theatrum* is given by DENUCÉ, ii, 92–148; of those of Mercator's *Atlas*, 1585–1637, by KEUNING (1947). Summary lists will be found in R. V. TOOLEY, *Maps and map-makers* (1949), pp. 30–33.

NOTES ON THE ILLUSTRATIONS

Plate 13   South-east Asia ('Asiae Tabula XI') in Mercator's edition of Ptolemy's *Geographia* (Cologne 1578 and 1584). Line-engraving. Size of original $13\frac{1}{2}''$ × 13″. Roman minuscules are used for the names of provinces, peoples, and gulfs; a fluent italic for other names. Mountains are drawn as overlapping cones, river sources as small ponds; the sea is stippled. The small strapwork cartouche and the rosettes at the corners are the only formal decoration, but 'voide places' in the sea are relieved by ships, on the land by local fauna.

Plate 14   Russia and central Asia, in Ortelius's *Theatrum orbis terrarum* (Antwerp 1570). Line-engraving by Frans Hogenberg from the map of Anthony Jenkinson, agent of the Muscovy Company in Russia; dedicated to Sir Henry Sidney. Size of original 14″ × 18″. The formal decoration is severe, but lively pictures of local inhabitants and animals are scattered over the map, with vignettes from Marco Polo. A triple scale gives Russian, English and Spanish miles.

Plate 15   The New World, 1587, in Ortelius's *Theatrum* (1590). Line-engraving. Size of original 14″ × 19″. With ornate strapwork cartouches and finely drawn ships. From New Guinea to Tierra del Fuego and the south Atlantic stretches the supposed Southern Continent. The narrow extension of the Pacific in longitude is noticeable.

Plate 16   Tartary or the Kingdom of the Great Khan, in Ortelius's *Theatrum* (1570). Line-engraving. Size of original 14″ × 19″. An elaborately decorated map, with an acanthus-leaf border, florid strapwork cartouches, and flourished italic capitals.

Plate 17   The Kingdom of Prester John or of the Abyssinians, in Ortelius's *Theatrum* (1573). Line-engraving. Size of original 15″ × 17½″. The lake-sources of the Nile are shown south of the Equator. The cartouches and lettering are ornate, the mountains and surfaces of the sea meticulously drawn.

Plate 18   The Holy Land, in Ortelius's *Theatrum* (1584). Line-engraving after Christiaan Sgrooten's map of 1570. Size of original 15″ × 20″. The sea, with swash lettering and a picture of Jonah and the whale, is represented by vivid wave forms, inland water by stippling. The border is a rope design, the strapwork cartouches are elaborately decorated with masks, medallions containing sacred scenes, fruit, feathers, birds, acanthus leaves. Scale in 'hours of travel'.

Plate 19   Byzantium, in the *Civitates orbis terrarum* of G. Braun, vol. I (Cologne 1573). Line-engraving by Frans Hogenberg. Size of original 13″ × 19″. The city is shown in bird's-eye view, and the surrounding landscape fancifully suggested. There is little ornament; Turkish figures are boldly drawn in the foreground.

Plate 20   Ancient Rome, in the *Civitates*, vol. II (1575). After a plan by Pirro Ligorio, 1553. Size of original 15″ × 20″. Engraved in a dry style appropriate to the classical subject.

Plate 21   Jerusalem, in the *Civitates*, vol. IV (1588). After a plan by Christiaen Adrichom. Size of original 14½″ × 19″.

Plate 22   Ostend, in the *Civitates*, vol. VI (1618). Size of original 13½″ × 18½″. The view shows the siege of the town by the Spaniards, 1601–4.

Plate 23   Title-page of *The Mariners Mirrour*, Anthony Ashley's English translation (London 1588) of the *Spieghel der zeevaert* by L. J. Waghenaer, the first printed sea-atlas. Size of original 13½″ × 9½″. New plates were engraved for the English edition by Hondius, de Bry, Ryther, and J. Rutlinger. The title-page, engraved by Theodore de Bry, is decorated with instruments of navigation: terrestrial and celestial globes, mariner's astrolabes, sand-glasses, cross-staff, lead-lines, and compass.

Plate 24   The coasts of England from Scilly to Plymouth, in *The Mariners Mirrour* (1588). Line-engraving by T. de Bry. Size of original 13″ × 20″. Cliffs are drawn in elevation; the coastal profiles are designed to identify the navigator's landmarks. Soundings and anchorages are indicated. Scale in English, Spanish and Dutch leagues. The fine quality of de Bry's decoration and lettering is seen in this and the two following plates.

Plate 25   Virginia, in Theodore de Bry's *America*, pt. I (Frankfort 1590). Line-engraving, from the MS. maps drawn by John White on Raleigh's colonising expedition in 1585. Size of original 12″ × 16″. The figures of Indians are also copied from White's drawings. The engraver's conventions distinguish ocean and enclosed waters and depict mountains in fanciful detail.

Plate 26   The West Indies, in de Bry's *America*, pt. IV (1594). Line-engraving. Size of original 13″ × 17″.

Plate 27   View of St Helena, engraved by Baptista van Deutecum, 1589, in J. H. van Linschoten's *Itinerario* (Amsterdam 1596, Dutch edition; 1599, Latin edition). Size of original 14½″ × 19½″. Linschoten's drawing shows a Portuguese squadron at anchor. The engraving is remarkable for its ornate formal cartouches and for the curious wave-pattern.

Plate 28   South America, in Linschoten's *Itinerario* (Dutch and Latin editions). Drawn and engraved by Arnold van Langeren. Size of original 15½″ × 22″. Two elaborate fretwork cartouches; roman and italic lettering in great variety; many drawings of natives and animals. Apart from reefs, which are stippled, the sea is blank. Scale (as on the other Linschoten maps) in German miles and Spanish leagues.

Plate 29   The Indian Ocean and south Asia, in Linschoten's *Itinerario* (Dutch and Latin editions). Engraved by Hendrik van Langeren. Size of original 15″ × 21″. This too shows much variety of lettering and a finely designed compass rose. The sea is blank.

Plate 30   The Arctic Regions, on a polar projection, engraved by Baptista van Deutecum, 1598, in Linschoten's *Itinerario* (Latin edition, 1599). Size of original 16½″ × 22″. The map was drawn by Willem Barents, who made three voyages (1594–7) in search of a north-west passage to the Indies; on the first he was accompanied by Linschoten. The track of the third voyage, on which Barents died, is shown; seals and whales abound in the ocean; the Magnetic Pole is drawn in 75°N. The flourished italic capitals are remarkable. The sea is blank.

v. The Beginning of
English Regional Cartography

(Plates 31–40)

The English, though backward in the processes of map-reproduction, did not lag behind other nations in the regional survey of their country. In 1575 a 'placart' of the Privy Council ordered that Christopher Saxton should be 'assisted in all places where he shall come for the view of mete places to describe certen counties in Cartes being thereunto appointed by her Ma^tes bill under her Signet'. This order, issued in the year after Saxton's first county maps were printed, is (apart from two grants of property) the earliest documentary record of the survey of the English and Welsh counties which he undertook by the command and at the expense of Thomas Seckford, an official of the Queen's court.

Saxton's was not the first project of the kind. An earlier proposal is found in a letter written in 1563 by Laurence Nowell, Dean of Lichfield, to his patron Sir William Cecil (later Lord Burghley), Secretary of State, 'complaining of the inaccuracy of the general maps of England, and stating his design of constructing maps of all the counties[1] if he should meet with Sir William's encouragement'. Saxton's enterprise, initiated by Nowell's friend Seckford, was more successful. Then as now, the defence of the Kingdom against enemies at home and abroad called for reliable maps, and official interest in the survey is indicated by the orders of the Privy Council issued in 1575 and 1576 to further it; by grants of land and rents made to Saxton; and by Burghley's receipt of early proofs[2] from the unfinished plates. Saxton's survey, conducted by summary methods, proceeded fast, and the 35 maps and frontispiece of his atlas were engraved between 1574 and 1579. If the dates of the engraved plates are taken as a guide, the survey began in East Anglia and the counties of the south and south-west, continued through the Midlands to northern England, and ended in the Welsh marches and counties.

English copper-plate engraving was still in its infancy; and the technique, for which metal-workers like Humphry Cole had a natural aptitude, was learnt by Englishmen from craftsmen of the Netherlands.[3] Fourteen of Saxton's plates are signed by Flemish or Dutch engravers, eight by English[4]; all 36 plates show the florid manner of conventional decoration and lettering practised in the Netherlands. Ryther indeed, in his Saxton maps, in the Armada charts of Robert Adams, and in his plates for *The Mariners Mirrour*, developed a mature style indistinguishable from that of his Flemish masters; but, like Cole, he called attention to his nationality in his signature – 'Augustinus Ryther Anglus'.

In 1577 Saxton obtained a ten-years' privilege to engrave, print and sell his maps, which from this date could probably be bought as separate sheets; and on their completion in 1579 they were issued as an atlas with a fine frontispiece, representing Queen Elizabeth as

---

[1] Two sets of manuscript maps by Nowell exist. His beautifully drawn regional maps, with Anglo-Saxon names, are in a British Museum MS., Cotton Dom. XVIII. 13; and Lord Lansdowne possesses a set bound in small format for use by Burghley as a travelling atlas.

[2] Now in the British Museum (Royal MS. 18. D.III), with annotations by Burghley and bound up with MS. maps used by him for political or military purposes. The rest of Burghley's map collection is still at Hatfield House.

[3] The first map engraved by an Englishman, that of the Holy Land by Cole (Pl. 31), illustrated the Bishops' Bible published by Archbishop Parker, in whose service Remigius Hogenberg was employed at this date (1572); and Cole may well have studied his craft under Hogenberg. The earliest town plan engraved by an Englishman is that of Cambridge (1574) by Richard Lyne, also a servant of Parker; and the engraved title-page of the Bishops' Bible has been attributed to Frans Hogenberg.

[4] The signed plates were engraved by Remigius Hogenberg (9), Leonhart Terwoort (4), Cornelis de Hooghe (1), Augustine Ryther (5), Francis Scatter (2), and Nicholas Reynolds (1).

the patron of astronomy and geography, and with an index. Saxton's was not the first detailed survey of a country, but his maps were acclaimed by contemporaries as a national atlas in which they could 'see all England set forth in several shires after the same manner as Ortelius hath dealt with other countries of the main, to the great benefit of our nation'.[1] William Harrison adds: 'For such hath been my help of maister Sackfords cardes, and conference with other men about these, that I dare pronounce them to be perfect and exact.'

With few changes,[2] Saxton's maps were frequently reprinted until Speed's county atlas, conceived on more popular lines, stole their market; but they were republished in 1645, with appropriate changes in the imprints and heraldry, to meet the demand for maps during the Civil Wars, and their later career can be traced in the imprints of the mapsellers into whose stock, in turn, the plates passed. The successive editions of the atlas are shown in the following list:[3]

1579–c. 1600	Editions sold by Saxton (and Ryther?)
1645	William Web. (Maps dated 1642)
1665	A projected edition, not completed, by an unknown publisher
c. 1683?	Philip Lea
1689	} Philip Lea
c. 1693	} (Roads and town plans added; many other alterations)
c. 1720	George Willdey
c. 1749	Thomas Jefferys
c. 1770	C. Dicey & Co.

Saxton's services to national cartography were completed by his wall-map of England and Wales (Pl. 34) engraved, on 20 plates, at Seckford's expense in 1583: 'a Description (wrote John Gregory in 1649) which . . . may compare with anie particular Table made . . . of anie Countrie whatsoever'. Although only two copies in the earliest state are now known,[4] the plates (like those of the atlas) had a phenomenally long life, and impressions from them, reworked and 'corrected', were on sale as late as 1795. During this span of 212 years they are found in the possession of Philip Lea, Thomas Bowles, John Bowles & Son, Robert Sayer, and Bowles & Carver.

John Norden, a lawyer whose adopted profession was estate management and survey, was less fortunate than Saxton in finding patronage for his county maps. His enthusiasm for 'chorography' (regional geography) led him, about 1590, to plan a series of county surveys for the traveller's pocket. These were designed to supply deficiencies which he had noted in Saxton's maps and Camden's descriptions:[5] roads, boundaries of hundreds,[6] town plans, historical sites and antiquities, a gazetteer of place-names, a reference grid, and a key to the symbols used (Pl. 35, 36). These details and aids to the map-reader had long been supplied by German cartographers, but Norden deserves the credit of introducing them in printed English maps. It is not improbable that some of his innovations were suggested to him by William Smith the herald and topographer, who had lived in Nuremberg for several years, and in whose manuscript surveys they are found; Smith's maps were not printed in his own day, but Norden and other cartographers are known to have had access to them.

---

[1] William Harrison, *Description of England* (1577).
[2] New indexes in a different order, additional preliminary pages, a few added place-names.
[3] Established by Dr Harold Whitaker.
[4] In the British Museum and Birmingham Public Library.
[5] William Camden, *Britannia* (1585).
[6] The hundreds (until the 19th century an important administrative division of the county) had been named and defined by Saxton in only five counties.

Norden's county handbooks, or 'chorographical descriptions', for which he chose the general title *Speculum Britanniae*, became a dominant preoccupation to which he returned in the intervals of other employment. Although he received a ten-years' privilege in 1593, no more substantial encouragement for his county surveys was offered him either by the Crown or by the eminent patrons to whom he dedicated his manuscripts and printed editions. The only two volumes of the *Speculum* printed in Norden's lifetime were published at his own expense. For Middlesex (1593), the maps and plans were engraved by a Fleming, Pieter van den Keere, Hondius's brother-in-law, then living in London; for Hertfordshire (1598), by an English engraver, William Kip (Pl. 35).

Besides the small maps of the *Speculum*, Norden drew a number of larger maps, of which three were printed – Surrey, Sussex (Pl. 36), and 'Hamshire'; and a splendidly written and illuminated manuscript dedicated to the Queen in 1595[1] contains maps, with abridged descriptions, of counties and islands surveyed on his travels through southern England. The ill-success of his county surveys is illustrated by the following lists of his surviving and lost works.

(a) *Speculum Britanniae* (text and maps)
Northants – MS. 1591; never printed. Another MS. 1610, now lost; printed 1720 without Norden's maps.
Middlesex – MS. (text only); printed (with maps) 1593, reprinted 1723.
Essex — Three MSS. (one with text only); printed 1840.
Hertfordshire – Two MSS.; printed 1598, reprinted 1723.
Cornwall – MS. (text only); printed 1728 without Norden's maps.

(b) *Queen's manuscript, British Museum Add. MS. 31,853* (abridged text and maps)
Middlesex, Essex, Surrey, Sussex, Hampshire, Isle of Wight, Guernsey, Jersey.[2]

(c) *Larger maps* (without text)
Surrey – Engraved by Charles Whitwell 1594.
Sussex – Engraved by Christopher Schwytzer 1595.
'Hamshire' – Engraver unnamed, *c.* 1595.

(d) *Lost or doubtful surveys*
Surrey – MS. now lost; recorded by R. Gough, *British Topography* (1780), ii. 261.
Kent – MS. now lost, also recorded by Gough, i. 441. The map in Camden's *Britannia* (1607) is signed 'Iohannes Norden deliniauit'.
Suffolk – Gough, ii. 257, says that Speed's map was 'augmented' from one by Norden.
Warwickshire – An anonymous map of 1603 has roads and other details which may be copied from a lost map by Norden, *c.* 1610.
Norfolk – An anonymous MS. description of Norfolk (printed 1938) has been attributed to Norden.

Norden's innovations, which left a lasting mark on the technique of map-drawing in England, were dictated by his practical sense as a topographer in recording, not mainly (like Camden) historical facts, but the contemporary face of the land, its towns and its people 'in their estate and forme as at this day they are'. His maps (when available) were copied, e.g. by Speed, in preference to those of Saxton, and for some counties his surveys held the field for nearly a century.[3]

[1] British Museum, Add. MS. 31,853.
[2] The maps of Middlesex, Surrey, and Sussex are now missing.
[3] The home counties – Middlesex, Surrey, Kent, Essex, Hertfordshire – were not re-surveyed until after 1670.

Four other collections of county maps, engraved near the turn of the century, deserve a brief notice. The earliest known pack of geographical playing-cards, published by an unidentified 'W. B.' in 1590, bore small maps of the English and Welsh counties (which by a happy chance numbered 52), copied from the general map in Saxton's atlas; for any county which Saxton combined with others on one plate, the playing-card of 1590 is the first separate printed map. In or about 1599, reduced copies of Saxton's maps were engraved by van den Keere for a projected 'pocket edition' of the atlas; this came to nothing at the time, but the plates were by 1627 owned by the publisher of Speed's *Theatre*, and they had a long career.[1] Another uncompleted project is represented by twelve unsigned county maps (two dated 1602, and one 1603) by an unidentified Netherlandish engraver. The maps, copied from Saxton and Norden, in the 1607 edition of Camden's *Britannia* were from plates by William Kip and William Hole, and this (with the possible but unimportant exception of the 1590 playing-cards) is the earliest 'atlas' engraved throughout by Englishmen.

John Speed, tailor and antiquary, designed his *Theatre of the Empire of Great Britaine* as a geographical prologue to the History for which, 'inspired by the zeale of my countries glory', he began to collect materials about 1596 or 1597. The *Theatre* was the first printed atlas of the British Isles; it dominated the English map-market in the 17th century, was republished towards the end of the 18th, and is still the most popular and familiar of early English atlases. Speed made little claim to originality for his maps, admitting 'I have put my sickle into other mens corne', and he tells us that 'the Chards for the most part traced by others . . . were the foundations of my begun pains; in supplying their wants with my many additions, and dimensions of the Shire-townes and Cities true platformes'. Although Speed shows no roads, those features of his maps in which he took special pride, such as hundred boundaries and town plans, are only an extension of Norden's ideas; but some at least of his 'additions' to the maps of Saxton and Norden were founded on first-hand information, for (he writes) 'the beautie and benefits [of our native land] not a farre off . . . but by my owne travels though every province of England and Wales mine eyes have beheld'. Plans of over 70 'cities and shire-towns' appear as insets of the county maps, and there is good reason to believe that three-quarters of these plans are Speed's own work.

Unlike Saxton and Norden, Speed sought no private employer; his patron was to be the map-buying public. The *Theatre*, both the title and arrangement of which followed the pattern of Ortelius's atlas, was designed to be a commercial success. Its maps incorporated popular decorative features wanting in those of Saxton, and it represented an ambitious capital investment by its publishers, John Sudbury and George Humble. Speed wrote that he 'saw the charges thereof (by others bestowed) to amount so high, as I held it a conscience[2] to frustrate their designments'. It is significant that the engraving, which began in or about 1605, was not entrusted to an English craftsman. All the plates were engraved in the Amsterdam workshop of Jodocus Hondius, whose signature is borne by 33 maps.[3] Both Speed and his publishers must have felt that so substantial a task called for the experience and industrial organisation of a Dutch firm, and the maps of the *Theatre* without doubt owe their success to Hondius's skill in the invention of picturesque decorative detail and in framing a coherent design from the heterogeneous drafts furnished by Speed.[4]

By 1608 the engraving seems to have been finished, except for minor details to be added by journeymen; most of the maps have the date 1610. The *Theatre* and *History* were published

---

[1] See below, pp. 55–56. [2] i.e. against his conscience.
[3] Hondius was well known in England from his residence in London, 1583–*c.* 1593. But an early version of Speed's map of Cheshire was engraved by William Rogers; it is possible that Rogers, who had associations with Sudbury and Humble, was to have engraved the whole series, but he died about 1604–5.
[4] See Introduction, p. 18.

together as a gigantic folio volume of 894 pages, with the date 1611 on the title-pages; but Books II–IV of the *Theatre* are dated 1612, the year in which printing was completed and the whole work published. The number of surviving copies of the 1611–12 *Theatre* suggests that a large edition was printed, and it at once eclipsed the popularity of Saxton's atlas. The text was newly set eight times from the first edition of 1611–12 to the last of 1676, but there were many more impressions of the plates, either in unaltered reissues of the text (till 1676), or for sale as separate sheets, or as an atlas without text (until about 1770). In successive alterations and additions to the plates we can trace their varying ownership (from the mapseller's imprint), fluctuations in public demand (from the reworking of worn plates), political changes (as when portraits of the Royal family, in the map of Scotland, are replaced under the Commonwealth by figures of peasants), and the incorporation of topical information (especially, from about 1700, roads).

The following list[1] summarises the bibliographical history of the *Theatre* with maps and text:

Publisher	Date of edition	Date on engraved title-page of *Theatre*	Text	State of maps
John Sudbury & George Humble	1611–12	1611	—	—
,,	1614–16	1614	Reset	Small changes
,,	1616		Latin	As 1614–16
George Humble	1623?	1614	Reissue of 1614–16 text	Ancient names (from Camden) added on most maps
,,	1627	1627	Reset	Generally as 1623
,,	1631–32	1627	Reset	New map of England
William Humble	1646	1627	Reset	Imprint changed on one map
,,	1650–54	1650	Five re-issues of 1646 text	Changes in date and imprint of certain maps
Roger Rea the elder and younger	1662	1650	Reset	Rea's imprint, other changes
Thomas Bassett & Richard Chiswell	1676	1676 (new plate)	Reset	Bassett & Chiswell's imprint, other changes

The later mapsellers who owned the plates and reprinted them with additions and alterations were Christopher Browne (*c.* 1690), John Overton (*c.* 1700), Henry Overton (from 1707), and C. Dicey & Co. (*c.* 1770). Of these, only Henry Overton (in 1743) and Dicey published the maps as an atlas.

From 1627 to 1676 two other atlases were published by George Humble and his successors in business as companions to the *Theatre*. Speed's *Prospect of the most Famous Parts of the World*, 'the first printed general atlas by an Englishman',[2] was printed in 1627, 1631, 1662 and 1676. Van den Keere's miniature plates after Saxton[3] were also acquired by Humble, who made up the set to 63 maps and issued it in 1627 as a pocket atlas for the shallower purse with the misleading title *England Wales Scotland and Ireland described and abridged . . . from a*

---

[1] Largely based on the research of the late Dr Eric Gardner.
[2] R. V. Tooley.   [3] See above, p. 54.

farr larger voulume done by John Speed.[1] This was regularly republished in the same years as the folio *Theatre*, and in 1646 William Humble produced a similar pocket edition of the *Prospect*, also with maps engraved by the aged van den Keere.

BIBLIOGRAPHY

SIR H. G. FORDHAM, *Studies in carto-bibliography, British and French* (1914).

SIR H. G. FORDHAM, 'Saxton's general map of England and Wales', in *Geogr. Journal*, lxvii (1926).

SIR H. G. FORDHAM, *Christopher Saxton of Dunningley* (1928).

SIR H. G. FORDHAM, *Some notable surveyors & map-makers of the 16th, 17th, & 18th centuries* (1929).

E. HEAWOOD, *English county maps in the collection of the Royal Geographical Society* (1932).

E. HEAWOOD, 'Saxton's large map of England', in *Geogr. Journal*, lxxvi (1930), 86–7.

T. CHUBB, *The printed maps of the atlases of Great Britain and Ireland, 1579–1880* (1927).

E. G. R. TAYLOR, *Tudor Geography, 1485–1583* (1935).

E. G. R. TAYLOR, *Late Tudor and early Stuart geography, 1583–1650* (1934).

R. FLOWER, *Laurence Nowell and the discovery of England in Tudor times* (1937).

E. LYNAM, *British maps and map-makers* (1944).

E. LYNAM, *An atlas of England and Wales: the maps of Christopher Saxton* (1939). (Introduction to the facsimiles published by the British Museum.)

E. LYNAM, 'English maps and map-makers of the 16th century', in *Geogr. Journal*, cxvi (1950).

H. WHITAKER, 'The later editions of Saxton's maps', in *Imago Mundi*, III (1939).

SIR H. ELLIS, Introduction to Norden's *Description of Essex* (1840).

W. B. GERISH, *John Norden* (1903).

A. W. POLLARD, 'The unity of John Norden', in *The Library*, new series, vi (1926).

G. R. CRONE, 'Early atlases of the British Isles', in *Book Handbook*, no. 6 (1948).

R. A. SKELTON, 'Pieter van den Keere', in *The Library*, series v, vol. v (1950).

SIR S. COLVIN, *Early engraving and engravers in England* (1905).

A. M. HIND, *Engraving in England in the 16th and 17th centuries* (in preparation).

Note: Many valuable catalogues of maps of individual counties have been published, notably by T. CHUBB and H. WHITAKER. There is a good bibliography of these catalogues in R. V. TOOLEY, *Maps and map-makers* (1949), pp. 72–74.

NOTES ON THE ILLUSTRATIONS

Plate 31　Detail from Humphry Cole's map of the Holy Land, published in the second edition of the Bishops' Bible, 1572. Original size. The first map known to have been engraved on copper by an Englishman, it is copied from Tilmann Stolz's map engraved by F. Hogenberg in the *Theatrum* (1570), with illustrations of the Exodus. The lettering (a neat, rather upright italic), the strapwork decoration and scrolls are in the Flemish manner. Mountains are shaded on the east, water features stippled. The 'complements' include the punning device (a nightingale in a thornbush) of the printer, Richard Jugge; the arms of Lord Burghley; a fourfold scale (of leagues, English and Italian miles, and the classical stadia) surmounted by a legend in a scroll stating that Italian and English miles each equal 1,000 paces; and the engraver's signature.

Plate 32　Staffordshire, by Christopher Saxton, engraved by Francis Scatter, 1577. Size of original $15\frac{1}{2}'' \times 20''$. This and Saxton's Cheshire are the only known work by Scatter, whose engraving and decoration stiffly imitate the Flemish style. The ring-fences indicating parks are noticeable. With the Royal arms and those of Thomas Seckford, as on all Saxton's maps.

Plate 33　Hampshire, by Saxton, engraved by Leonhart Terwoort of Antwerp, 1575. Size of original $16'' \times 17\frac{1}{2}''$. One of the five Saxton maps signed by Terwoort, who uses characteristic Flemish lettering and ornament, with an individual bent for naturalistic detail.

[1] Only the text and 23 new maps were copied from Speed.

Plate 34   Plate 17 of Saxton's large map of England and Wales, 1583. Perhaps engraved by Augustine Ryther, whose work in Saxton's county maps and the Armada charts it recalls. Size of original 11″ × 17″. The reproduction is made from the British Museum copy, in which the separate sheets are bound as a volume. This sheet includes Cornwall and the lower part of the threefold scale, in long, middle and short ('longa, mediocria, parva') miles, of which 50, 55 and 60 respectively make a degree of latitude. In the stippled sea are well drawn ships, including a fishing vessel from which men are dragging up nets. Latitude and longitude are marked in the margin, and a legend records that the prime meridian is the easternmost island of the Azores.

Plate 35   Hertfordshire, by John Norden, engraved by William Kip, 1598. Size of original 7½″ × 9½″. In Norden's *Speculi Britanniae Pars. The Description of Hartfordshire*. Roads are denoted by double dotted lines, hundred boundaries by a single 'pricked' line. The battle of Barnet is represented by clashing soldiers, although in his Middlesex (1593) Norden had used a cross for a battle site. The margin has two-mile divisions, lettered and numbered for reference, as in earlier German maps (cf. Pl. 10b), whose conventions are recalled by Norden's symbols.

Plate 36   Detail of Sussex, by John Norden, engraved by Christopher Schwytzer, 1595. Original size. The finely drawn plan of Chichester is enclosed in a scroll. Norden's table of symbols is seen, and there is a marginal scale of miles. Beachy Head is drawn in elevation. The engraving and decoration are in the Flemish style. The arms are those of William Sanderson, merchant adventurer, who financed the making of Molyneux's globes. His arms also appear on Norden's map of Hampshire.

Plate 37   Anglo-Saxon Britain, in John Speed's *Theatre of the Empire of Great Britaine* (London 1611–12). Size of original 16″ × 21″. Engraved by Jodocus Hondius from the map engraved by William Hole in Camden's *Britannia*, 1607 edition. Speed has added fourteen vignettes of the early Anglo-Saxon Kings, and their coats of arms.

Plate 38   Surrey, in Speed's *Theatre*. Size of original 16″ × 21″. Signed by Hondius 1610. After Norden's map of 1594, with the addition of coats of arms of Earls and two vignettes; but Norden's roads are omitted. The views of the Royal palaces are drawn in a foreshortened perspective; that of Richmond is copied from a drawing by A. van Wyngaerde.

Plate 39   Middlesex, in Speed's *Theatre*. Size of original 16″ × 21″. Signed by Hondius 1610. The county map and plans of London and Westminster are copied from Norden's Middlesex, 1593; roads are omitted from the map. The two cathedrals, like the Royal palaces of Surrey, betray the hand of Speed's (anonymous) architectural draughtsman. Hondius has built the details into a symmetrical design; his calligraphic fancy is seen in some striking flourishes, and his taste for naturalistic ornament in the two birds (a hoopoe and a rook) supporting a Roman coin above the imprint panel.

Plate 40   Cambridgeshire, in Speed's *Theatre*. Size of original 16″ × 21″. Dated 1610. Copied from Saxton's map, with additions. The decoration and 'compartments' which crowd in on the map include the nobly engraved Tudor Royal arms and those of the University and its colleges and of Earls and Dukes; figures in academic costume, one holding the scale; and a plan of Cambridge, copied from that of John Hamond engraved in 1592. In spite of the small scale, the names are not crowded; the italic and roman lettering are neatly combined and contrasted.

VI. Dutch and German Map-Publishers
17th and 18th Centuries
(Plates 41, 43–66, 70–78)

By 1600 Ortelius, Frans Hogenberg, and Mercator were dead; Antwerp had lost its primacy in the Netherlands map-trade, in which Plantin's heirs were no longer active; and that of the Rhineland had passed its first spring.[1] The leadership of the cartographic industry in north-west Europe moved to Amsterdam, the school of Dutch pilots and the base for the overseas enterprises by which Holland was to build her commercial empire in the 17th century. The service of the Dutch East and West India Companies provided work in plenty for chart-makers: Peter Plancius played an active part in founding these companies, and W. J. Blaeu and his son held in succession the appointment of hydrographer to the East India Company. Merchants, growing rich with the prosperity of Dutch trade, became connoisseurs and collectors of finely decorated maps and atlases; and the technical skill developed in drawing and engraving charts for navigators was applied to satisfy the 'curiosity of amateurs'.[2] Here we see the two aspects of the great Dutch map-publishing industry which dominated the European market throughout the 17th century: on one hand, scientific and practical work for seamen – on the other, the commercial manufacture of atlases and wall-maps to furnish the libraries of dilettanti.

It was to Amsterdam that, after about ten years' exile in London, the Flemish engraver Jodocus Hondius, accompanied by his brother-in-law Pieter van den Keere (Petrus Kaerius), moved about 1593. During their residence in England, which encouraged the development of native engraving, Hondius had engraved, among other works, charts in *The Mariners Mirrour* (1588) and the first English globes, those of Emery Molyneux completed in 1592; and van den Keere had worked for Norden (1593). Hondius's workshop at Amsterdam seems to have expanded rapidly; in or about 1605 he began the engraving of the maps for Speed's *Theatre*, which were finished by 1610; and in 1606 he published a new edition of Mercator's *Atlas*, the first of many to appear over his imprint. The nucleus of this was the 107 original Mercator maps (102 by Gerard, 5 by his sons), the copper plates of which Hondius had purchased in 1604; to these he added 36 new maps (Pl. 43–48). After his death in 1612, publication of the atlas was continued by his widow and younger son Henricus; and by 1632 twenty editions[3] had appeared, with the Mercator maps and a steadily growing number of new plates, and the Mercator-Hondius atlas had successfully driven Ortelius's *Theatrum*[4] out of the market. Now it had to face a new rival.

Willem Janszoon Blaeu[5] had about 1596 set up in business as a maker of instruments and globes, and later as engraver and printer. The mathematical and practical bent of his genius is apparent throughout his work. His earliest publications were declination tables, charts and sailing directions for pilots, and his services to navigation were recognised by grants from the States General and by his appointment (in 1633) as map-maker to the

---

[1] But at Cologne the sixth and last volume of the *Civitates* came out in 1618, and Matthias Quad published atlases, mainly copied from the *Theatrum*; and at Frankfort the work of de Bry and his sons was continued by their successor Matthäus Merian, the founder of the great series of German 'town-books' entitled *Topographia Germaniae*.

[2] Gregorii (1713).

[3] Thirteen with Latin text, seven with French. Henricus's imprint first appears on the title-page in 1623.

[4] The last edition of which appeared in 1624.

[5] Until about 1619 Blaeu signed with his patronymic 'Willem Jansz.', 'Guilielmus Janssonius', and similar forms; and writers of his own day and later (e.g. Gregorii) have often confused him with his competitor Jan Jansson, the successor to Hondius's business.

Republic. To the organisation of his printing house Blaeu applied no less technical ingenuity. He is known in the annals of typography as the inventor of an improved printing press, which increased the printer's output by a quarter;[1] and a well-known description of the printing house which he built in 1636–7 (a year before his death) indicates the highly developed workshop organisation of Blaeu and his sons. Filip von Zesen, who visited Amsterdam in 1663, wrote:[2] 'On the Blumengracht . . . may be found the far-famed printing-house of Johan Blaeu . . . It is equipped with nine type presses, named after the nine Muses, six presses for copper-plate printing, and a type foundry.' Zesen goes on to describe the storage cases for the copper plates 'from which the atlases, the town-books of the Netherlands and other foreign countries, the sea-atlases and other choice books are printed'; the press-rooms for plate- and book-printing; the rooms for proof reading, washing type, and drying the sheets. To these processes must be added the drawing and engraving of maps, the making of the fine paper with Blaeu's own mark, and the binding in vellum covers. Blaeu's correspondence shows that the head of the business, himself a craftsman, directly controlled every stage in the production of his maps and books.

The firm of Hondius and its associates had early entered into commercial competition with this formidable rival. In 1608, the year in which Hondius published a large world map with features borrowed from Blaeu's of 1605, Blaeu appealed to the States General for protection against persons who robbed him of his livelihood by copying his maps; and between 1620 and 1637 Jan Jansson, Hondius' son-in-law, produced over his own imprint pirated editions of Blaeu's sea-atlas *Het Licht der zeevaert*. The later development of the Mercator-Hondius atlas tells of imitation and copying from that of Blaeu. Yet it is an evident if unexpected fact that Hondius, Blaeu, Jansson, Visscher and other map-publishers collaborated with one another by the sale or loan of plates and impressions or by executing work on contract.[3]

The early history of Blaeu's atlas provides a curious instance of this. Unlike Hondius, he possessed no large stock of atlas maps round which to construct his atlas. About 1629 he purchased 37 plates from Jodocus Hondius the younger, and most of these (with altered imprints) were included in the prototype of his world atlas, the *Atlantis Appendix* of 1630.[4] To meet this threat to its market, a much enlarged edition of the Mercator-Hondius atlas, in two volumes, was brought out in 1633; the preface, which contained slighting references to Blaeu's compilation, was signed by Henricus Hondius and his brother-in-law Jan Jansson,[5] and 28 maps bore Jansson's imprint.

In 1635 Blaeu's atlas was published in two volumes, with editions in four languages; and for the next thirty years the rival atlases ran a parallel course, expanding *pari passu* in imitation of each other, with that of Hondius (published from 1638 by Jansson alone) usually lagging. By 1660 Jansson's *Novus Atlas*, with Latin text, extended to eleven volumes; and Blaeu's magnificent *Geographia Blaviana*, or *Atlas Major*, was issued in nine to twelve volumes, with over 600 maps and separate editions in Latin, German, Dutch, French, and Spanish.[6]

---

[1] 'The New-fashion'd Presses [those of Blaeu] are used generally throughout all the Low-Countries' (Joseph Moxon, 1683).
[2] *Beschreibung der Stadt Amsterdam* (1664), pp. 215–6.
[3] Cf. Introduction, p. 7, note 4; and Wieder, *Monumenta Cartographica*, iii (1929), p. 69.
[4] Only two copies are known.   [5] Jansson was the son of an Arnhem printer.
[6] The editions of the Mercator-Hondius-Jansson atlas are described by J. Keuning, 'The history of an atlas', in *Imago Mundi*, IV (1947) and VIII (1951); those of the Blaeu atlas by F. C. Wieder, *Monumenta Cartographica*, iii (1929), pp. 69–77. Short lists are given by R. V. Tooley, *Maps and map-makers* (1949), pp. 32–35.

The story of their fourth volume, containing maps of the British Isles mainly copied from Speed, illustrates the competition between the two atlases. About 1640 both publishers set about the preparation of this volume. Jansson already had at his disposal eighteen 'British' plates which had previously been printed in the Hondius atlas, and in 1644 he added eleven more; but Blaeu was ready first, and his volume (which omitted Scotland) came out in 1645. Six of his 59 maps were copied from those of Jansson, the remainder from Speed. Jansson's volume, which appeared in the following year, shows signs of hasty production; there are many mistakes in pagination, the printing and presswork are poor, ten maps represent pairs of counties, and six Welsh counties have no map. Ten of Jansson's 62 maps were copied from those of Blaeu, and he evidently revised his plates after the appearance of Blaeu's maps, all of which had coats of arms copied from Speed; none of Jansson's maps published down to 1644 had the coats of arms, which were, however, added to them before publication in 1646. The fifth volume of Blaeu's atlas, issued in 1645, contained maps of Scotland drawn from the sketches of Timothy Pont, and is the first printed atlas of that country (Pl. 61).

Competition in atlas-building plainly did not encourage original work in cartography; old plates, or plates copied from earlier maps, were freely used to fill out a volume, and map-makers, working against time to supply the presses, had little leisure for critical study of their sources or for revision of their outlines.[1] The atlases of Blaeu, Jansson, Visscher, Danckerts, de Wit, and later publishers were not compiled, like that of Mercator, from scrupulous research nor, like that of Ortelius, with acknowledgement to the cartographers whose work was reproduced. But the popularity of the decorative maps in these atlases lent them an often undeserved authority as geographical documents.

The maps added by the elder Hondius to the earlier editions of his atlas (Pl. 43–48) were engraved in the bold and swaggering style popular about 1600. The formal cartouches are not elaborate and the borders are undecorated, but a great variety of roman and italic lettering is used, with fantastic flourishes, the sea is covered with heavy 'shot-silk' shading, and mountains stand out in strong relief. The later work of Jansson (Pl. 51–54) and of Blaeu (Pl. 55–61) is altogether different in intention and appearance. The drawing of geographical features is much refined, if little more trustworthy; place-names are engraved in a neat and uniform italic letter, and calligraphic flourishes are rare. From the point of view of map-design, these are marked improvements, which may perhaps be credited to Blaeu. The exercise of decorative or playful fancy was confined to the groups of figures supporting cartouches, to heraldic ornament (Pl. 52, 59), and to title-pages, and reaches its apogee in Jansson's splendidly flamboyant version of the title-page of Speed's *Theatre* (Pl. 53).

The houses of Hondius, Jansson and Blaeu commanded the commercial market in the first two-thirds of the 17th century; but other engravers, some of whom began their career with these firms, engaged in map-publishing. Claes (Nicolaes) Jansz. Visscher, after working for Hondius, set up his own printing-house, which was in turn inherited by his son (from 1637) and grandson (from 1679), both of whom bore the same names.[2] The son, who produced large wall-maps in the manner of Blaeu and published his first atlas in 1666, is commended by Gregorii as a good geographer who often passed whole days without meals while working on his maps; their drawing, he adds, is 'the clearest and neatest of any maps we have'. Cornelis Danckerts engraved a map of the battles and civil wars of Britain for the 1627 edition of Speed's *Theatre*, and his son Justus founded a family publishing house which

[1] See Introduction, p. 9.
[2] Their dates are: C. J. Visscher I, 1587–1637; II, 1618–79; III, 1649–1709. They used the same signature, but the son sometimes latinised his name on his maps – 'N. J. Piscator'.

from about 1670 issued a series of gradually enlarged atlases.[1] Gregorii draws attention to the decoration and colour of maps by Danckerts and records that 'his clear engraving and illumination attracted many collectors who bought all his maps whether they were accurate or inaccurate'. Both the Visscher and Danckerts family were outrun in production and in contemporary reputation by the great house of Frederik de Wit (father, son, and grandson of the same name), which between 1648 and 1712 produced, in Gregorii's estimate, 410 new maps, besides republishing earlier plates in their possession.

By 1670 or 1680 the running had been taken up from the Blaeu and Jansson firms by other map publishers, and the later history of the Dutch map-trade may be traced in the transfer of older plates from one printing house to another, with alterations of imprints and other changes. After Jansson's death in 1664 his business was carried on by his two sons-in-law under the name Janssonius-Waesbergh; and in 1694[2] they sold the plates by auction. Those of the atlas fell to their former employee Pieter Schenk and his partner Gerard Valk, and those of the 'town-books' (including the old plates of the *Civitates*) to Frederik de Wit.[3] Joan Blaeu's printing house was destroyed by fire in 1672, and the surviving plates were bought by de Wit. De Wit's whole stock passed on his death in 1706 to Pieter Mortier,[4] who also acquired from Schenk the old Jansson plates. Schenk meanwhile had, soon after 1712, purchased the Visscher business from the widow of C. J. Visscher III.

In the early 18th century the Dutch map-trade was thus concentrated in the hands of a group of large publishers, notably Schenk (1660–1718/19), Karel Allard (1648–1706), Danckerts and Mortier. Quantity was the keynote of their production and, while old plates were sometimes 'scrapped' or sold,[5] new maps were largely copied from those of Sanson and other French cartographers. A characteristic product of the period is the enormous *Galerie agréable du monde*, published by Pieter van der Aa in 1729 and containing over 3,000 plates in 66 volumes.

The handsome Dutch sea-atlases of the 17th century have a bibliographical character somewhat different from that of the land-atlases. Charts are more subject to revision and have a smaller sale than land-maps; the sea-atlases were accordingly produced in smaller editions, and the plates had a shorter life than those of the land-atlases. In the first half of the century Blaeu's two collections, *Het Licht der zeevaert* and *De Zeespieghel*, were frequently reprinted; and the fifth volume of Jansson's atlas, added in 1651, was a sea-atlas. After 1650 many other publishers entered this field;[6] their work, unlike Blaeu's, was often designed less as aids to navigation than as collectors' pieces for libraries. The charts in these sea-atlases are finely engraved and coloured, with elaborate naturalistic decoration round the cartouches; and the title-pages (the plates of which sometimes served more than one atlas) are florid compositions with vignettes, allegorical figures, instruments and other ornaments in fantastic baroque arrangements surrounding the title (Pl. 64). The illumination in the atlases of Pieter Goos, a cousin of the Hondius family, is especially fine (Pl. 65). The *Neptune français* (1693), engraved by Romein de Hooghe, illustrates the close relations between the French and Dutch map-trade at the end of the century; the edition with French text was

---

[1] The active dates of the Danckerts family help in dating atlases containing the imprints of different members. Cornelis, 1603–56; sons of Cornelis – Dancker, 1634–66; Justus, 1635–1701; sons of Justus – Justinus (?); Theodorus, 1660–1727; Cornelis, 1664–1717.

[2] After a commercial flirtation with the English publisher Moses Pitt, for whose uncompleted *English Atlas* (1680–83) many of Jansson's plates were used.

[3] Second of the name.

[4] First of the name (active 1685–1719). His son and grandson bore the same name; the firm, under the style Covens & Mortier, continued to publish throughout the 18th century, and only ceased work in 1866.

[5] For instance to England; see pp. 8, 71.

[6] A convenient list of Dutch sea-atlases is given by R. V. Tooley, *Maps and map-makers* (1949), pp. 36–7.

published by A. H. Jaillot at Paris, those with Dutch and English texts by Pieter Mortier at Amsterdam and his son David Mortier at London respectively.

The German map-trade was in the 17th century mainly dependent on that of Holland. There was a vigorous native output of plans and views of towns, for which the great series of topographical works produced at Frankfort by the Merian family, the successors of de Bry, set the fashion. But Amsterdam was the principal source from which the German market was supplied with maps. In the absence of an organised native industry, Germans in fact found it cheaper to buy the Dutch maps either at the book-fairs of Frankfort and Leipzig or from travelling colporteurs, as Gregorii (writing as late as 1713) makes plain. A few German engravers learned their profession in Amsterdam and, like Jakob von Sandrart who was apprenticed in the workshops of Danckerts and Hondius, returned to Germany to produce copies of Dutch and French maps; others, like Schenk, a Saxon by birth employed by Jansson's heirs, remained in Amsterdam to found their own printing businesses.

The first German map-engraver to found a printing house ('officina') comparable with those of the Netherlands was J. B. Homann of Nuremberg (1664–1724). After early activity as an engraver he set up his publishing business in 1702, and the commercial organisation of his workshop enabled him to build up a stock of atlas-plates and to sell his work at lower prices than those of the French and Dutch maps from which it was for the most part copied.[1] Homann's commercial success effectively restored the self-respect of German cartography. He himself was in 1715 appointed Geographer to the Emperor; his printing house was frequented by geographers; and under his successors J. C. Homann (1703–30) and J. M. Franz (1700–61), who used the imprint 'Homann'sche Erben', it became a centre for academic geographical studies and for cartographic reform. The history of this house is a striking illustration of the essential service which a commercial map-publisher may provide for scientific geography; yet the conservative element in the copper-plate map industry is illustrated by the fact that in 1770 more than half the stock of the 'Homann heirs' consisted of the original plates engraved by J. B. Homann. Franz estimated in 1747 that of some 16,000 land-maps in existence not more than one-ninth were original; he added that the map-production of the various publishers was 'a continual plagiarism' and that the purchaser of a 'new' map bought nothing but a new title. After Nuremberg, the most prolific centres of the German cartographic industry in the 18th century were Augsburg, where the active but less original firms of Matthäus Seutter and the Lotter family were established; and Vienna, where the house of Artaria dominated the market at the end of the century.

BIBLIOGRAPHY
(See also the Bibliographies to Chapters IV and V)

F. C. WIEDER, *Monumenta Cartographica* (1925–34).

J. KEUNING, *Petrus Plancius* (1946).

J. KEUNING, 'The history of an atlas: Mercator-Hondius', in *Imago Mundi*, IV (1947).

E. HEAWOOD, *The map of the world on Mercator's projection by Jodocus Hondius, Amsterdam 1608* (1935).

J. KEUNING, 'Jodocus Hondius Jr.', in *Imago Mundi*, V (1948).

P. J. H. BAUDET, *Leven en werken van W. J. Blaeu* (1871).

E. L. STEVENSON, *Willem Janszoon Blaeu . . . a sketch of his life and work* (1914).

J. KEUNING, 'Hulpmiddelen bij de dateering van verschillende uitgaven van W. J. Blaeu', in *Tijdschrift van het Kon. Nederlandsch Aardrijkskundig Genootschap*, dl. lvii (1940).

J. KEUNING, 'The Novus Atlas of Joannes Janssonius', in *Imago Mundi*, VIII (1951)

[1] J. Hübner in 1726 gave the relative prices of maps in Hamburg as follows: German, 4–5 Groschen; Dutch, 5–6; French, 6–7; and English, 7–8 Groschen.

VI. DUTCH AND GERMAN MAP-PUBLISHERS

P. A. TIELE, *Nederlandsche bibliographie van land- en volkenkunde* (1884).

A. M. LEDEBOER, *De boekdrukkers, boekverkoopers, en uitgevers in Noord-Nederland* (1872).

E. W. MOES, *De Amsterdamsche boekdrukkers en uitgevers in de 16e eeuw* (1896–1915).

M. M. KLEERKOOPER and W. P. VAN STOCKUM, *De boekhandel te Amsterdam in de 17de eeuw* (1914–16).

F. G. WALLER, *Biographisch woordenbook van Noord-Nederlandsche graveurs* (1938).

J. G. GREGORII, *Curieuse Gedancken von den . . . Alt- und Neuen Landcharten* (1713).

H. ECKARDT, *Matthäus Merian: Skizze seines Lebens und . . . Beschreibung seiner Topographia Germaniae* (1887).

C. SANDLER, 'Johann Baptista Homann', in *Zeitschrift der Gesellschaft für Erdkunde in Berlin*, xxi (1886).

C. SANDLER, 'Die homännischen Erben', in *Zeitschrift für wissenschaftliche Geographie* (1890).

E. D. HAUBER, *Versuch einer umständlichen Histoire der Land-Charten* (1724–26).

J. HÜBNER, *Museum Geographicum, das ist: ein Verzeichniss der besten Land-Charten* (1726).

J. G. DOPPELMAYR, *Historische Nachricht von den Nürnbergischen Mathematicis und Künstlern* (1730).

C. SANDLER, 'Matthäus Seutter und seine Landkarten', in *Mitteilungen des Vereins für Erdkunde* (1894).

NOTES ON THE ILLUSTRATIONS

Plate 41   The Seventeen Provinces of the United Netherlands in the form of a lion, in *Germania Inferior* by Petrus Montanus, engraved and published by Pieter van den Keere (Amsterdam 1617). Size of original 14½″ × 17¾″. A symbolic representation, copied from the engraving by Frans Hogenberg in Michael Aitsinger's *Leo Belgicus* (1582). Colour is applied in outline to emphasise the design.

Plate 43   Fez and Morocco, in the Mercator-Hondius *Atlas* (Amsterdam 1606). Size of original 14½″ × 19″. One of the new plates added by Hondius and copied from Ortelius's map. The engraving is heavy and flamboyant, the italic lettering profusely flourished.

Plate 44   China, in the Mercator-Hondius *Atlas* (1606). Size of original 13½″ × 17″. Also added by Hondius.

Plate 45   Japan, in the Mercator-Hondius *Atlas* (1606). Size of original 13½″ × 17″. Copied by Hondius from Ortelius's map.

Plate 46   South America, in the Mercator-Hondius *Atlas* (1606). Size of original 14½″ × 19″. Also added by Hondius.

Plate 47   Virginia and Florida, in the Mercator-Hondius *Atlas* (1606). Size of original 13½″ × 19″. Copied by Hondius from the map in de Bry's *America*, pt. I (1590), engraved from John White's drawings. The vignettes of Indian villages are also copied from engravings by de Bry after White.

Plate 48   Cuba and Hispaniola (Hayti), in the Mercator-Hondius *Atlas* (1606). Size of original 14″ × 14½″. One of the new plates by Hondius.

Plate 49   New England, 'observed and described by Captain John Smith, 1614', engraved by Simon van de Passe at London about 1616. Size of original 12″ × 13¾″. The ninth state, with the imprint of James Reeve, London, and with the arms of the Council of New England added above the compass rose. Inserted in this state in Wye Saltonstall's version of the Mercator-Hondius atlas, *Historia Mundi or Mercator's Atlas*, published at London in 1635 with the small plates of Hondius's *Atlas Minor* (1607 and later editions), and reprinted in 1637. The map, a sophisticated example of Flemish engraving, is decorated by Smith's portrait (perhaps drawn from the life by van de Passe), the Royal arms (top) and those of Smith (bottom left).

Plate 50 Virginia, engraved by Ralph Hall, 1636. Size of original 6¾″ × 9½″. A crude copy from William Hole's engraving of Captain John Smith's map of Virginia, first published in 1612 and frequently reprinted. The engraver, who gives his own name to 'Hall poynt' (not found on any other map), unskilfully imitates Flemish conventions of drawing and decoration, and has copied his vignettes from de Bry. This map also was added to Wye Saltonstall's *Historia Mundi*. In the Errata of the 1635 edition we are told that 'there is no Map of Virginia in regard there is a more exact Map drawing in that Country, whose Platforme is not yet come over'; Hall's map may be assumed to have been inserted to supply this deficiency.

Plate 51 The East Indies, in the Mercator-Hondius *Atlas* (1633); the second state, with the imprint of Jan Jansson. Size of original 13½″ × 18″. Engraved in the neater manner introduced by Blaeu and Jansson.

Plate 52 Essex, in Jansson's *Novus Atlas*, vol. IV (Amsterdam 1646). Size of original 15″ × 19½″. The plate, copied from the map in Speed's *Theatre*, was first printed, with Jansson's imprint, in the German edition (1633) of the Mercator-Hondius atlas; in this (the second) state the coats of arms, also copied from Speed, have been added.

Plate 53 Title-page of Jansson's *Novus Atlas*, German edition, vol. IV (1647). Size of original 16¼″ × 9½″. First published, with Latin text, in 1646. The title and imprint are engraved; a label bearing the German title is pasted over the original Latin title, and the imprint date has been altered on the plate. The design represents a baroque façade. The vigorously drawn figures of a Briton, a Roman, a Dane, a Saxon and a Norman are freely adapted from those on the title-page engraved by Hondius for Speed's *Theatre* and *History*.

Plate 54 The Atlantic Ocean ('Mar del Nort'), in Jansson's *Novus Atlas*, vol. V (1650). Size of original 17″ × 22½″. As usual in early charts, direction lines radiate from the main compass rose and from centres arranged on the circumference of a circle round it. The cherubs round the scale cartouche play with a surveyor's chain.

Plate 55 Valois, in the first edition of Blaeu's *Novus Atlas* (Amsterdam 1635), vol. I. Size of original 15½″ × 19½″. The geographical outline and detail are copied from the map in Le Clerc's *Théâtre géographique* (1619), which was drawn with east at the top. Blaeu has re-oriented his map; there is no compass rose, but the four cardinal points are written in the border. The drawing is more precise than that of the French map, and symbols and lettering are neatly subordinated to the geographical features. The finely engraved decoration includes the arms of the province (top right) and a group of hunters round the title panel.

Plate 56 America, in Blaeu's *Novus Atlas* (1635), vol. I. Size of original 16½″ × 22″. As in Blaeu's wall-maps of the continents, the border is filled with vignettes containing views of towns and groups of natives.

Plate 57 New Belgium and New England, in Blaeu's *Novus Atlas* (1635), vol. II. Size of original 15¼″ × 19¾″. Derived from a MS. map of 1614 probably by Adriaen Block, with additions from the map in J. de Laet's *Nieuwe Wereldt* (1630 edition). West is at the top of the map. The interior is decorated by pictures of local fauna, and the vignettes of Indian villages are copied from de Bry.

Plate 58 Brazil, in Blaeu's *Novus Atlas* (1635), vol. II. Size of original 14¾″ × 19¼″. Copied from a map in Joannes de Laet's *Nieuwe Wereldt ofte Beschryvinghe van West-Indien* (1625). West is again at the top.

Plate 59   The Territory of Frankfort, in Blaeu's *Novus Atlas* (1640), vol. I. Size of original 18″ ×
21½″. This map, added to the first three-volume edition of the atlas, published after the
elder Blaeu's death, is evidently designed as an ornamental piece. There is no border, and degrees of
latitude and longitude are not marked. The exuberant decoration arranged round the map includes
symbolic figures and the arms of the Frankfort magistrates.

Plate 60   Tierra del Fuego and the Straits of Magellan, in Blaeu's *Novus Atlas* (1640), vol. II. Size
of original 16¼″ × 21″. This map, with its more correct outline of 'Magellanica', was
introduced in place of an old plate copied by Jodocus Hondius the younger from de Laet and published
in earlier editions of the Blaeu atlas. Drawn on the Mercator projection, the map has a chequer-board
scale showing the number of German miles in each increasing degree of latitude.

Plate 61   Isle of Arran, in Blaeu's atlas, vol. V (1654). Size of original 15″ × 20½″. The maps of
Scotland in this volume were engraved after the drafts made by Sir Robert Gordon of
Straloch from the rough sketches of Timothy Pont, who surveyed most of Scotland before 1610. The
hills are varied in form and size. The cartouches are framed in shell-work designs and brightly coloured.
On the face of the map colour is used only for outlining boundaries and bringing hills into relief.

Plate 62   'Old and New Virginia', in Sir Robert Dudley's *Dell'Arcano del Mare* (Florence 1646–7),
Book VI. Engraved by A. F. Lucini. Size of original 19″ × 14½″. Dudley's *Arcano*, the earliest
sea-atlas with all the charts drawn (about 1636) on the Mercator projection, and the first engraved
sea-atlas by an Englishman, is rich in hydrographical data. This chart, the outline of which is derived
from Captain John Smith and other sources, records soundings, sand-banks and reefs (represented
by stippled lines), and magnetic variation, and has notes on winds and currents. The Tuscan engraver
uses a strong line for coasts and a calligraphic and highly flourished script.

Plate 63   The Coast of Guiana, in Dudley's *Dell'Arcano del Mare*, Book VI. Engraved by A. F. Lucini.
Size of original 18½″ × 28½″. For this chart, first printed (as his text states) in 1637, Dudley's
principal source was his own voyage to Guiana in 1594–5.

Plate 64   Title-page of *De Zee-atlas, ofte Water-weereld*, by Pieter Goos (Amsterdam 1666). Size of
original 15½″ × 9″. A characteristic example of the elaborate title-pages of Dutch sea-atlases.
Above a moulded pediment is Urania, the Muse of Astronomy, surrounded by cherubs 'shooting' the
stars with cross-staffs; round the shellwork frame of the title are arranged globes, an armillary sphere,
a compass, a quadrant, and other instruments; at the foot, above the imprint, curtains are drawn back
to disclose a 'sea-piece' representing a naval battle. This plate was also used by Goos for his *Zee-spiegel*
(1662).

Plate 65   Detail (the east coast of England) from the chart of the North Sea in Pieter Goos's *Zee-atlas*
(1675). Original size. The coasts, as in most Dutch charts of this period, are outlined in red,
reefs in brown. The agricultural decoration of the cartouche represents the occupations of the inhabitants.

Plate 66   The Coast of Guinea, in Johannes van Keulen's *Zee-atlas* (Amsterdam 1681; English edition
1682). Size of original 20½″ × 23½″. The coasts are represented by a double line, shaded in
colour; rocks and soundings are intermittently marked. On an awning stretched between two trees
is the title, surrounded by an animated group of figures representing a merchant trading with natives.

Plate 70   The Island of Negroponte, by Vincenzo Maria Coronelli, *c.* 1690. Size of original 10½″ ×
17″. (The ornamental border is omitted.) A *bravura* design, in which a map of the island and
a view of the city are linked by a decorative device. Coronelli, Cosmographer to the Republic of
Venice, was the foremost Italian cartographer of his day, whose virtuosity was matched by his prodigious
output.

Plate 71   Candia (Crete), by Frederik de Wit, *c.* 1680. Size of original 18″ × 21¼″. The treatment is
        pictorial; the border represents a moulded frame, the insets are carefully balanced, and the
map lacks scale, compass indicator, and graduation. Fortifications are emphasised both in the title
and on the map insets.

Plate 72   Star chart of the Southern Hemisphere calculated for the year 1700, by Karel Allard. Size
        of original 19¾″ × 22¾″. In the margins are maps of the Sun and the Moon and a diagram
of a total eclipse of the sun, 14 May 1706. The figures of the constellations in celestial charts offered an
ample opportunity for decorative treatment and for colour.

Plate 73   New Belgium, New England, Virginia, by Justus Danckerts; with a view of New York,
        'lately called New Amsterdam'. Size of original 18½″ × 21¾″. Copied from a map by C. J.
Visscher, itself derived from a prototype map by Jansson of *c.* 1660. The view, which first appears on
Visscher's plate, is from a water-colour of *c.* 1670; the gallows-like structures in the foreground are a
crane and (probably) a weighing-apparatus. When this plate was first engraved and published is
unknown; this impression must be later than 1682, as Philadelphia (founded in that year) has been
added to the map and the details of Pennsylvania have been re-engraved.

Plate 74   Zealand (Denmark), in the *Atlas Contractus* of Pieter Schenk (Amsterdam, *post* 1713). Size
        of original 17½″ × 21″. This is a Jansson plate acquired by Schenk and Gerard Valk about
1683. In the imprint Jansson's name has been replaced by those of Schenk and Valk, in the dedication
by that of Schenk alone.

Plate 75   Dunkirk and Mardyck, published by Anne Beeck at The Hague, *post* 1713, and included in
        Schenk's *Atlas Contractus*. Size of original 15½″ × 18″. The plan, which indicates the fortifica-
tions demolished and the harbour filled in under the terms of the Treaty of Utrecht (1713), is designed
to show the new canal constructed by Louis XIV after the Treaty.

Plate 76   The World, by Gerard and Leonard Valk; engraved *c.* 1690 and included by Schenk
        (who had been in partnership with G. Valk) in his *Atlas Contractus*. Size of original 18¾″ ×
22¼″. The elaborate and gaily coloured mythological decoration round the map is etched.

Plate 77   Profile view and plan of Barcelona, published by Karel Allard, *post* 1697, and included
        in Schenk's *Atlas Contractus*. Size of original 8¾″ × 10¾″. The legend records the restoration
of the town to Spain by the Peace of Ryswick, 1697. Here, as often in military maps of the 17th and
18th centuries, the fortifications are drawn in plan, other features in bird's-eye view.

Plate 78   The Harbour and Straits of Gibraltar, published by Karel Allard, *post* 1704, and included
        in Schenk's *Atlas Contractus*. Size of original 19½″ × 23″. Showing the capture of the fortress
by the combined English and Dutch fleet, July 1704.

VII. French Cartography
17th and 18th Centuries
(Plates 79–81)

A national tradition in cartography can establish itself only with difficulty if machinery for the publication of maps does not exist or is imperfectly developed. In France, as in England, the independent trade in prints and maps was late in hiving off from that in books; and many notable maps and charts by French cartographers of the 16th century remained in manuscript, or became known by editions printed in Italy or the Netherlands. The first atlas of the French provinces, *Le Théâtre Françoys* (1594), was produced by a bookseller, Maurice Bouguereau, at Tours, then the refuge of the royal court and of many members of the Paris book-trade. Bouguereau's atlas, like Speed's, imitated the *Theatrum* of Ortelius both in its title and method of compilation, and his engraver Gabriel Tavernier was probably a Protestant expatriate from Antwerp, where his son is said to have been an apprentice of Ortelius.

France achieved political stability later than England, and there was at this date no strong central government which could order a national survey like Saxton's and secure its completion. The earliest French regional atlas was necessarily a collection of maps by various cartographers, only a few being printed for the first time. Bouguereau's plates were acquired, and new maps were added to them, in turn by Jean Le Clerc, who republished them in three atlases (1619, 1620, 1621) under the title *Théâtre Géographique du Royaume de France*, by Le Clerc's successors (editions of 1622, 1626, 1631), and by Jean Boisseau (*Théâtre des Gaules*, 1642). Melchior Tavernier, the son or brother of Gabriel, published an atlas under the same title as that of Le Clerc (editions of 1634 and 1637), in which his own plates were supplemented by impressions from those of other French or Dutch engravers.

The establishment of the royal authority under Louis XIV created the conditions in which an independent French map industry could develop as a 'productive unit'[1] comparable with the great Dutch industry centred in Amsterdam. Map-making, in common with fine and applied arts generally, enjoyed royal patronage and was harnessed to the service of the State; and cartography of the 17th and 18th centuries in France had an 'official' character scarcely known in other countries. Nicolas Sanson of Abbeville, the first great cartographer of this period, was 'géographe ordinaire du roi', as were most of his successors. In the 17th and 18th centuries the output of French graphic and decorative artists, working in a tradition of neo-classical baroque design, achieved great beauty and distinction; and the map-makers of France profited by the accomplishment of her copper-plate engravers and type-designers.

As Sir George Fordham remarked, Sanson (who was at first associated with Melchior Tavernier) and his engravers were almost all 'either Flemings or of the neighbouring province of Picardy', but his maps have an individual and wholly French elegance in the drawing of their detail and the character of their lettering. Sanson's maps, which were first collected in atlases from about 1645, were exported and liberally copied by Dutch, English, and German cartographers until the early decades of the 18th century. After his death in 1667 his business was carried on by his sons, from whom it was acquired by A. H. Jaillot. Jaillot, whose family printing-house survived until 1780, re-engraved the Sanson maps for a series of splendidly decorated atlases, the first of which, the *Atlas Nouveau* dedicated to the Dauphin, appeared in 1689 and was reissued by Mortier at Amsterdam and London from 1696. Material from Sanson's workshop was incorporated as late as 1757 in the *Atlas Universel* of Gilles Robert de Vaugondy and his son Didier.

[1] Sir G. Fordham.

These map-houses, although they did not ignore original and up-to-date information in their new maps, may be said to represent the commercial and conservative element in French cartography. Although outside the scope of this book, the great contemporary advances made by the French in scientific geodesy and survey must be briefly recorded. The 'reformation of cartography'[1] due to French geographers, mainly under the auspices of the Académie des Sciences, is marked by several stages. The basic task was the computation of the shape and circumference of the earth; and Jean Picart's measurement of an arc of a meridian in 1669–70 was the first of a series of such operations by French scientists. Members of the Académie, using a method for determining longitude devised by Jean Dominique Cassini, director of the Observatory of Paris, established the correct position of a large number of places by astronomical observation. These advances enabled French cartographers to re-draw the map of the world, purging it of the gross errors in longitude which had hitherto distorted it, and to construct a scientific map of France. The reform of the world map was mainly the work of Claude Delisle and his more famous son Guillaume, and of J. B. Bourguignon d'Anville. Guillaume Delisle's maps, published from about 1700 in the successively enlarged editions of his *Atlas Nouveau*, incorporated the data furnished by geodesists and astronomers; and d'Anville carried the reform into its final stage, erasing from the map all unauthenticated detail long accepted by more credulous cartographers and admitting only information which could survive the test of his searching criticism. The great map of France, the earliest map of any country constructed on a firm basis of geodetic calculation and accurate survey, was the work of J. D. Cassini's son César François Cassini de Thury, who completed the triangulation of the country in 1744 and began to prepare the maps, on a scale of about $1\frac{1}{3}$ miles to an inch, about 1750 (Pl. 81).

The French cartographers of the 18th century, introducing new standards of accuracy in the compilation of their maps, were no less original in adapting their design to the expression of geographical facts. The graceful cartouche of Delisle's map of Canada (Pl. 79) and the charming *chinoiserie* of the ornament in d'Anville's *Nouvel Atlas de la Chine* (Pl. 80) have a decorative beauty unsurpassed in the maps of any period; but the engraver has not allowed his fancy to elaborate the face of the map, where we find no intrusive decoration. The formal but elegant lettering of place-names and legends, carefully graded, recalls that of contemporary French typography. Geographical features, on both small- and large-scale maps, are drawn with precision and clarity; and the conventional signs, employed by Cassini in rich variety, instantly evoke the features which they represent. French map-makers of this period excelled in devising appropriate and accurate symbols for the features of physical and human geography; and to them we owe the introduction of contour lines for relief.[2] The representation of relief, it may be noted, is the weakest aspect of Cassini's map. Although he substitutes vertical shading for the conical hills still shown in perspective by Delisle and d'Anville, his shading is drawn only to mark the limits of river valleys, so that the whole countryside appears to have two levels only – that of the valley floor and that of the remaining tableland – divided by an escarpment.

BIBLIOGRAPHY

L. Drapeyron, 'Le premier atlas national de la France, 1589–1594', and 'L'évolution de notre premier atlas national sous Louis XIII', in *Bulletin de géographie historique et descriptive* (1890).

Sir H. G. Fordham, *Studies in carto-bibliography* (1914), chap. VII, 'The cartography of the provinces of France, 1570–1757'.

[1] C. Sandler's phrase.   [2] See Introduction, p. 13.

VII. FRENCH CARTOGRAPHY

Sir H. G. Fordham, *Some notable surveyors & map-makers of the 16th, 17th, & 18th centuries and their work* (1929).

Sir H. G. Fordham, 'Notes on a series of early French atlases, 1594–1637, presented to the British Museum', in *The Library* (1921).

C. F. Roland, *Alexis-Hubert Jaillot, géographe du roi Louis XIV* (1919).

C. Sandler, *Die Reformation der Kartographie um 1700* (1905).

L. A. Brown, *Jean Domenique Cassini and his world map of 1696* (1941).

E. Doublet, 'Une famille de géographes et d'astronomes: De l'Isle', in *Revue de géographie commerciale* (1934).

C. F. Cassini, *Description géométrique de la France* (1783).

H. M. Berthaut, *La carte de France 1750–1898* (1898–9).

H. M. Berthaut, *Les ingénieurs géographes militaires 1624–1831* (1902).

NOTES ON THE ILLUSTRATIONS

Plate 79   Canada, by Guillaume Delisle, 1703. Line-engraving. Size of original 19¾″ × 26″. The map, included in various editions of Delisle's *Atlas Nouveau*, is here reproduced from a later state, in which the date has been deleted from the title panel. Covens & Mortier, whose imprint is added to this state of the map, published Delisle's atlas at Amsterdam, and his plates became their property. In the singularly fine decoration of the cartouche, French colonial administration is symbolised by the Royal arms and figures of a priest and a lawyer. The map is drawn on a conical projection and longitude is reckoned from Ferro, in the Canaries. Mountains and rivers are, as in all Delisle's maps, deliberately emphasised. Long legends discuss doubtful geographical points.

Plate 80   The province of Kwei-chow, in d'Anville's *Nouvel Atlas de la Chine* (The Hague 1737). Line-engraving. Size of original 10½″ × 12″. The maps in this atlas were prepared by d'Anville from those of the Jesuit missionaries who surveyed China for the Emperor K'ang-hsi in 1708–16. The Jesuit maps were brought to Paris by Père J. B. du Halde, whose *Description de la Chine* d'Anville's atlas accompanied. Besides the draft maps, du Halde probably supplied d'Anville with the material from which the 'Chinese' decoration of the maps was engraved.

Plate 81   Detail from sh. 22 of *Atlas topographique des environs de Paris* (Paris 1768). Line-engraving. Original size. Part of the Cassini map of France on a scale of about 1⅓ miles to the inch, this map illustrates its design and conventions. Relief is somewhat weakly represented by vertical shading indicating the edge of river valleys. The plan of parks and forests is carefully laid down in full detail. The symbols show great variety and delicacy of drawing; larger towns are drawn in plan. The colouring is strictly functional; main roads are in red, secondary roads in yellow. The *Atlas* was published by the successor of R. J. Julien, agent for the sale of Cassini's map, whose stock is stated in an advertisement on the title-page to include 4,000 maps.

VIII. English Cartography
17th and 18th Centuries
(Plates 67–69, 82–84)

When Speed published his *Theatre*, the 'Tudor discovery of England' had already spent its initial force. Apart from 'promotion' maps[1] and estate survey, little original work in cartography was done in the early and middle decades of the 17th century. The demand for 'war maps' during the Civil Wars was supplied by reprints from the old plates, or by copies, of the county maps of Saxton, Norden and Speed, or of road books such as the *Direction for the English Traviller* (1635).[2]

By the Restoration the time was ripe for a re-discovery of England. As Celia Fiennes wrote, 'if all persons . . . would spend some of their tyme in Journeys to visit their native Land . . . it would form such an Idea of England, add much to its Glory and esteem in our minds and cure the evil itch of overvaluing foreign parts'. Although Pepys used Speed's atlas in reconnoitring the Forest of Dean for ship-timber, the Elizabethan surveys and the Dutch maps derived (through Speed) from them were inadequate as a topographical basis for the enterprises which sprang up in many fields of national effort. New agricultural crops and methods were introduced, and inland waterways constructed; the turnpike system was instituted, and a postal service established; ports grew with the extension of overseas trade and plantation; statistical surveys and town planning schemes were undertaken; antiquarian studies flourished; the Royal Society was incorporated, and the Navy reorganised. The Restoration opened a fresh epoch in English cartography. The new threads which it wove into the old pattern included the revival of English marine hydrography, hitherto dependent on the Dutch; John Adams's attempted re-survey of the country on geodetic principles; the publication of gazetteers;[3] new surveys of individual counties by John Ogilby, John Seller, Robert Plot and others; the mapping of roads and standardisation of distance measurement; the measurement of longitude from the London meridian; and the rapid growth of the print- and map-selling trade.

Roads took on special importance from the development of highway law. They were now drawn on almost all new maps and added to the old copper plates of Saxton and Speed still in use. When not derived from survey, they were copied from the strip maps in Ogilby's road-atlas, *Britannia Vol. I* (1675),[4] which were drawn from measured survey on a scale of one inch to a mile. This was part of Ogilby's projected 'English Atlas', in which he 'Design'd to each Quarter of the Globe one fair volume, and a fifth to Britannia'. His Africa, Asia and America were published; but of the second and third volumes of Britannia, to be devoted to a series of city plans and to a 'topographical description' of the country, only the plans of London and Westminster and three county maps[5] reached print (Pl. 69).

Ogilby was concerned with 'the Post Roads for conveying Letters missive to and from this Great Center [London]', and his preface discusses the units of measurement in current use, which are also displayed in the threefold scale of the map of England prefixed to the

---

[1] Connected with civil engineering schemes such as the draining of the Fens. The craft of estate surveys was developed with advances in mathematical technique in this century.

[2] The first English road book with maps, and the earliest county atlas in which all the counties are drawn on the same scale.

[3] Most of these, even Adams's famous *Index Villaris* (1680), were based on the lists of places printed on the back of the maps in Speed's *Theatre*.

[4] The earliest complete set of county maps to show the roads (from Ogilby) was a pack of geographical playing-cards published by Robert Morden in 1676.

[5] Kent, Middlesex (Pl. 69), Essex.

road maps: the 'vulgar computed' mile of customary reckoning, the 'direct horizontal' mile calculated from the map, and the 'dimensurated road' mile of 1,760 yards from his own survey with the 'Wheel Dimensurator' half a pole (2¾ yards) in circumference. The mile of 1,760 yards had been prescribed for London and Westminster by a statute of 1593 and, with the spread of the postal service from London in the 17th century, came to be accepted as the post-mile for the kingdom; Ogilby's was the first atlas to employ it consistently.[1]

Other contemporary map-publishers laid plans for an 'English Atlas', no less rich in promise but even poorer in performance than that of Ogilby.[2] John Seller, primarily a maker of charts and instruments, projected an 'Atlas Anglicanus',[3] for which the maps of only six counties were completed (1676–80), although it is said that 'King Charles and King James II chose him to Survey the several Counties'.[4] The county maps in Richard Blome's *Britannia* (1673) and his *Speed's Maps Epitomiz'd* (1681) were crudely drawn reductions from those of Speed. The maps prepared by Robert Morden for the new English translation of Camden's *Britannia* (1695) and claimed to be 'by much the fairest and most correct of any that have yet appear'd', were, although only in part from survey, revised from local information, and this is the first collection of county maps to use the prime meridian of London throughout.[5]

The business and organisation of London printsellers expanded in scope and complexity after the Restoration; but the English market for maps and especially charts was still dependent on the output of Amsterdam firms. Relations between the Dutch and English trades were close: Dutch map-engravers settled in London,[6] Amsterdam publishers like Mortier had a London office and imprint, and Dutch maps (both sheets and copper plates) were imported in great numbers.[7] The uncompleted *English Atlas* (1680–83) of Moses Pitt was substantially a collection of Jansson's maps printed (at Amsterdam) from the original plates, with altered imprints, under a contract between Pitt and the Jansson heirs.[8] Christopher Browne had his imprint engraved on the de Wit plates which he purchased; and, as Pepys noted, John Seller printed his sea-charts from 'the old worn Dutch copper plates' which he had bought 'for old copper' from de Wit, Danckerts, Visscher and others. In the county atlases sold by John Overton before he acquired the Speed plates about 1700, impressions from plates in his own possession (e.g. those of the twelve anonymous maps of 1602–3) were supplemented by Jansson or Blaeu maps imported from Holland for his stock.

Seller, Overton and Philip Lea were the most substantial London map-publishers at the end of the 17th century; and into their hands passed the stock and goodwill of most of the older firms. The printing of a new edition from old plates was often a joint-stock enterprise. Lea, who worked in association with Morden, Seller, Seller's successor John Thornton, and others, included in his stock the plates of Saxton's large map of England and county

[1] The 'statute mile' was eventually established by the Act for the Uniformity of Measures (1824), but 'old miles' of various lengths have remained in use within living memory.

[2] See E. G. R. Taylor, 'Robert Hooke and the cartographical projects of the late 17th century', in *Geographical Journal*, xc (1937).

[3] In the British Museum there is a preliminary model of this atlas, with the MS. title *A Collection of the County Mapps of the Kingdome of England and Principality of Wales*, and containing maps by Speed, Jansson, and Seller himself. The counties surveyed by Seller were Hertfordshire, Surrey, Middlesex, Kent, Buckinghamshire, and Oxfordshire.

[4] Camden, *Britannia Abridg'd* (1701). This work contains a set of smaller county maps by Seller.

[5] The first map on which this prime meridian is adopted seems to be Seller's Hertfordshire (1676).

[6] e.g. Herman Moll, who was in London by 1678, in association with Moses Pitt. See Robert Hooke's Diary, ed. 1935, p. 377; and J. N. L. Baker, 'The earliest maps of H. Moll', in *Imago Mundi*, II (1937).

[7] See Introduction, p. 8.

[8] E. G. R. Taylor, 'The English Atlas of Moses Pitt', in *Geographical Journal*, xcv (1940). Only one map was certainly 'designed, drawn, and engraved' in England.

maps, which he revised and reissued, adding roads (from Ogilby) and town plans (from Speed). Overton acquired Speed's plates from Christopher Browne about 1700 and his son Henry gradually revised them, altering the imprint and adding roads, until his definitive edition of 1743. Seller's shop in the City dealt in land-maps and instruments for survey and navigation; but his main business, carried on at Wapping, the centre of hydrographical activity from Tudor times, was in the production of charts and sea-atlases. Here, in 1671, he began the publication of *The English Pilot* (Pl. 67) which, over the successive imprints of Seller, Thornton, Richard Mount, Mount & Page, Mount & Davidson, and Smith & Vennor, was reprinted in many editions until the early 19th century.[1] But the earliest English sea-atlas engraved from original surveys, Captain Greenvile Collins's *Great Britain's Coasting Pilot* (1693), was published by Mount (Pl. 68).

After the Hanoverian settlement English cartography developed on independent lines, and economic conditions in the map-trade no longer checked, but encouraged, original work. The growth of country estates and changes in methods of cultivation and land tenure created security of employment for the surveyor. His principal masters were still the landed gentry whose houses and parks, with their owner's names and coats of arms, were laid down on the county maps of the 18th century. Nor, in a period of commercial expansion and political rivalry, was there any want of official patrons for both marine and land surveyors at home and oversea. The Army and Navy, government offices like the Board of Trade and Plantations, colonial Governors and chartered Proprietors, all had need of accurate maps. Able English surveyors, such as William Mayo, sought their opportunities in the American colonies, and their work (Pl. 83, 84) was engraved and published by London mapsellers like Senex and Jefferys, whose output thus acquired a semi-official character recognised by the appointment of Geographer to the King. By the middle of the century there was also a vigorous demand for county maps, and estate surveyors had extended their practice to the survey of counties, which was encouraged by premiums offered by the Society of Arts. Gough selects four such craftsmen for special mention: 'Surveys on large scales were reserved for the labours of a Rocque, a Jefferies, and a Taylor, and a Chapman.[2] – I invert the chronological order for the climax of merit' (*British Topography*, vol. i, p. xvi). The county maps of these men (Pl. 82) reflect their experience in surveying estates and parks; the ownership and layout of properties, the character of cultivation and land-surfaces, and sometimes even field boundaries are indicated, by conventions derived (notably in Rocque's maps) from those of contemporary French cartography.

The ornament of maps was increasingly subordinated to topographical and antiquarian information supplied in vignettes and long engraved legends, as in Bowen and Kitchin's *Large English Atlas*, or in symbols of ever wider variety. Decoration was concentrated in the borders and cartouches, which in the late 17th century were framed in complex designs of shellwork, fruit and flowers reminiscent of contemporary stucco ornament on buildings, and in the 18th century reflected the conventions of local rococo design. Lettering, in which the English 'copper plate' round hand predominated, became more utilitarian and related to its function.[3]

[1] A useful list of the volumes and editions of *The English Pilot* is given by R. V. Tooley, *Maps and mapmakers* (1949), pp. 60–61. Other English sea-atlases are listed by Tooley, pp. 61–64.

[2] The following counties were mapped, on scales of one inch to the mile or larger, by these surveyors: John Rocque – Shropshire, Berkshire, Middlesex, Dublin, Surrey (all published between 1752 and 1770); Thomas Jefferys (with collaborators) – Staffordshire (1747), Bedfordshire, Durham, Huntingdon, Oxford, Buckinghamshire, Yorkshire, Northants (all between 1765 and 1779); Isaac Taylor – Hereford, Hampshire, Dorset, Worcestershire, Gloucestershire (all between 1754 and 1777); John Chapman – Nottinghamshire (1776), Essex (with Peter André or Andrews, 1777).

[3] e.g. the grading of towns: 'Ye Markett Towns are Distinguish'd by Round Roman Hand' – John Oliver's map of Essex, 1696.

The demand for the services of surveyors and for their maps brought to the map-trade the capital and the market which it needed for expansion. In the 18th century we hear of the export of English maps to the Continent, and by the time of Jefferys this trade was well established.[1] The leading houses engaged in all the cartographic processes from survey to publication. Some, like those of Overton and Bowles, did not confine themselves to topographical subjects but produced, in addition, engraved work of great variety;[2] others, like those of Senex, Jefferys, and Cary, dealt almost exclusively in maps. Some of the firms, which under their successive proprietors (from the end of the 17th to the end of the 18th century) had the largest output and longest life, are shown in the following notes:[3]

Thomas Bowles (fl. 1702–64)[4] acquired part of the stock of Philip Lea, including the plates of Ogilby's county maps, and of John Seller (the county maps but not the hydrographical material). His business in St Paul's Churchyard passed to his grandson *Carington Bowles* (1724–93) and after the latter's death was continued under the style *Bowles & Carver* (1794–1832). In 1795 this firm was selling impressions from the plates of Saxton, Seller, Lea, John Adams, H. Moll, Senex, Emanuel Bowen, Thomas Kitchin, Rocque, Jefferys, and other earlier cartographers.

John Bowles (fl. 1720–79), the son of Thomas and father of Carington, founded a separate shop in Cornhill, in which for eleven years (1753–64) he was in partnership with Carington under the style *John Bowles & Son*. It was taken over after his death in 1779 by *Robert Wilkinson* (fl. 1779–1829), who seems to have transferred his interest, about 1794, to *Bowles & Carver*.

John Overton (fl. 1663–1713), who had acquired from his predecessor Peter Stent plates by Norden, Symonson and other Tudor cartographers, sold his stock in 1707 to his son *Henry Overton* (fl. 1707–58). This included the original Speed plates which were about 1770 in the possession of the bookseller *C. Dicey*.

Philip Overton (fl. 1720–51), another son of John, set up a separate business, mainly for the production of charts, at first alone and from 1745 in partnership with Robert Sayer.

Richard Mount (fl. 1684–1722) acquired Seller's hydrographical stock, including the plates of *The English Pilot*, from his successors *John Thornton* and *Samuel Thornton*. His business was carried on by his son *William Mount* (died 1769) at first alone and then, under the style of *Mount & Page*, in partnership with Thomas Page (died 1762). They were succeeded by their sons John Mount and Thomas Page the younger; and the firm was continued into the 19th century under the names (in succession) of *Mount & Davidson* and *Smith & Vennor*.

John Senex (fl. 1690–1740), besides his large trade in land maps, is said to have acquired some of Seller's hydrographical plates. His business was acquired from his widow in 1745 by

Robert Sayer (fl. 1745–94), already part-owner of Philip Overton's stock. This firm continued under the successive styles of *Robert Sayer*, from 1751 to 1770; *Sayer & Bennett*, 1770 to 1784; *Robert Sayer*, 1784 to 1794, when the business was taken over by *Robert Laurie* and *James Whittle*. (The modern firm of Imray, Laurie, Norie & Wilson Limited

---

[1] See above, p. 10.
[2] e.g. prints of historical, military and naval subjects; 'sporting-pieces'; engraved writing- and drawing-books; religious and humorous prints; mezzotint portraits; games and 'school-pieces'.
[3] Based on the biographical notices in Chubb, *A Bibliography of Printed Maps* (1927), and on a card index in the Map Room of the British Museum, supplemented by other sources.
[4] A genealogical table of the Bowles family is given by Sir G. Fordham, *Hertfordshire Maps* (Supplement, 1914), p. 5.

was formed in 1903 by a merger of the three chart-publishing houses of R. H. Laurie, Imray & Son, and Norie & Wilson.)

Emanuel Bowen (fl. 1720–67) was succeeded by his son *Thomas Bowen* (died 1790), most of whose stock came into the hands of Bowles & Carver.

Thomas Kitchin (fl. 1738–84), whose stock was dispersed on his death; some of his plates were later in the possession of Bowles & Carver.

John Rocque (c. 1704/5–62), most of whose stock seems to have been acquired from his widow by Carington Bowles and Robert Sayer.

Thomas Jefferys (fl. 1732–71), who was succeeded in business by *William Faden* (1750–1836), although a few of his plates were acquired by other mapsellers. Faden's business was continued in the 19th century by *James Wyld*, father and son.

In 18th-century England, as in 17th-century Holland, the expansion of the map market not only encouraged new work based on original survey, but also prolonged the life of old copper plates. In the catalogues of 18th-century mapsellers we find, in curious juxtaposition, the old maps of Saxton, Hollar, Seller, and John Adams side by side with county maps or road books from the newest surveys or traverses. Plagiarism too was as common in the cartography as in the literature of the period; Gough's remark[1] that 'as to the several sets of county maps professing to be drawn from the *latest* observations, they are almost invariable copies of those that preceded them', may be compared with Dr Johnson's, that 'those who fill the world with books . . . have often no other task than to lay two books before them out of which they compile a third, without any new materials of their own'. Nevertheless, in an abundance of chaff there was much good grain; and the county maps of Rocque, Chapman and André, and Jefferys, the work of colonial and military surveyors in North America, and the marine surveys of James Cook and the hydrographers of the East India Company, are a not unfitting prelude to the age of official cartography in which the Ordnance Survey and the Hydrographic Department of the Admiralty took up the running.

BIBLIOGRAPHY

(See also the Bibliography to Chapter V)

R. GOUGH, *British topography* (1780).

SIR H. G. FORDHAM, *Some notable surveyors & map-makers of the 16th, 17th, & 18th centuries* (1929).

SIR H. G. FORDHAM, *Hand-list of catalogues and works of reference relating to carto-bibliography for Great Britain and Ireland, 1720 to 1927* (1928).

SIR H. G. FORDHAM, *The road-books and itineraries of Great Britain, 1570 to 1850* (1924).

SIR H. G. FORDHAM, *John Ogilby, 1600–1676. His Britannia and the English itineraries of the 18th century* (1925).

T. CHUBB, *The printed maps of the atlases of Great Britain and Ireland, 1579–1880* (1927).

H. WHITAKER, *The Harold Whitaker Collection of county atlases, road-books & maps presented to the University of Leeds* (1947).

R. V. TOOLEY, *Maps and map-makers* (1949). Lists of English marine atlases, pp. 60–64; of English county maps, pp. 75–79; and of carto-bibliographies of individual counties, pp. 72–74.

E. LYNAM, *British maps and map-makers* (1944).

BIBLIOGRAPHICAL SOCIETY, *Dictionary of printers and booksellers . . . in England, Scotland and Ireland, 1668–1725*, by H. R. Plomer (1922); *1726–1775*, by H. R. Plomer, G. H. Bushnell, and E. R. McC. Dix (1932).

E. ARBER, *The Term Catalogues, 1668–1709* (1903–6).

J. DUNTON, *The life and errors of John Dunton* (1705). Racy reminiscences of book- and print-sellers of the late 17th century.

[1] Gough singles out Bowen and Kitchin for special censure in this respect.

H. Whitaker, 'The later editions of Saxton's maps', in *Imago Mundi*, III (1939).

E. Heawood, 'John Adams and his map of England', in *Geographical Journal*, lxxix (1932).

E. G. R. Taylor, 'Robert Hooke and the cartographic projects of the late 17th century', in *Geographical Journal*, xc (1937).

E. G. R. Taylor, 'Notes on John Adams and contemporary map-makers', in *Geographical Journal*, xcvii (1941).

E. Wilson, *The story of the blue-back chart* (1937). History of the firm of Imray, Laurie, Norie, & Wilson Limited and its predecessors.

J. Varley, 'John Rocque, engraver, surveyor, cartographer, and map-seller', in *Imago Mundi*, V (1948).

W. B. Crump, 'The genesis of Warburton's map of Yorkshire 1720', in Thoresby Society's *Miscellanea*, xxviii (1948); and 'The road surveys of John Warburton', in *Transactions of the Halifax Antiquarian Society* (1926). Field-books and other records of an 18th-century county survey.

G. Kish, 'The correspondence of continental mapmakers of the 1770's and 80's with a London firm [Jefferys and Faden]', in *Imago Mundi*, IV (1947).

W. Lowery, *The Lowery Collection* (1921). Contains notes on the Faden Collection of MS. maps, now in the Library of Congress.

Sir H. T. Wood, 'The Royal Society of Arts. – VI. The Premiums (1754–1851)', in *Journal of the Royal Society of Arts*, lx (1912).

Sir C. Close, *The early years of the Ordnance Survey* (1926).

E. D. Fite and A. Freeman, *A book of old maps delineating American history* (1926).

P. L. Phillips, *A list of maps of America in the Library of Congress* (1901).

H. N. Stevens, *Lewis Evans: his Map of the British Colonies in America* (third edition, 1924).

NOTES ON THE ILLUSTRATIONS

Plate 67   The Coasts of Northern Europe, in *The English Pilot*, book I (1671), by John Seller. Size of original 17¼″ × 21″. Copied from a Dutch chart, whose ornament and figures are clumsily reproduced by the English engraver. The goat in Scandinavia, the sledge with reindeer, and the whaling group in the Arctic Ocean were conventional decorations in 17th-century maps of the northern regions.

Plate 68   Chart of Dartmouth with an inset of Torbay, by Captain Greenvile Collins, in *Great Britain's Coasting Pilot* (London 1693). Size of original 11¾″ × 22½″. The hydrographic features include soundings, anchorages and rocks. Shore landmarks, e.g. churches, are drawn in elevation, as if laid on their back, for easy recognition; sight-lines are laid down as an aid in entering the estuary; and coastal profiles are provided in a separate panel (bottom right). The symbolic ornament of the cartouches includes fishing nets and lobster pots. The map is dedicated to Pepys's patron Lord Dartmouth and displays his arms.

Plate 69   Detail of John Ogilby's map of Middlesex, engraved by Walter Binneman, *c.* 1677. Original size; scale about ¾″ to a mile. A variety of symbols distinguish villages and hamlets of different types, and large houses are drawn in elevation, as are the rows lining the streets of towns. Roads and bridges are conspicuous. Woods are indicated by single trees.

Plate 82   Detail (Kensington) from John Rocque's *Survey of London and Westminster and the country . . . round*, engraved by Richard Parr in 1746. Original size; scale 5″ to a mile. Rocque's earlier works were plans of parks and gardens, and in this map he applies a similarly formal technique to the representation of land-surface and use. Parks are precisely drawn in plan; suitable conventions, recalling those of estate maps, distinguish ornamental gardens and nurseries, plantations and orchards, cultivated land and waste. The darker aspect of 18th-century London is suggested by the gallows and 'Stone where Soldiers are Shot' at Tyburn (Marble Arch).

Plate 83   Plan of the City of New York (south sheet), with a S.W. view of the city. Surveyed in 1766–
67 by Lieutenant Bernard Ratzer, 6oth Regiment; engraved by Thomas Kitchin and published in 1776 by Jefferys & Faden, London. Size of original 22¾″ × 37″. Thomas Jefferys died in 1771, but William Faden continued to use the joint imprint for several years, and included this plan in his *North American Atlas* (1777). The map, with its indication of plot boundaries and cultivation and its pictorial symbols for plantations and hedges, exemplifies the preoccupation of the military surveyor, as of the estate surveyor, with land surface. The decoration of the finely engraved cartouche symbolises the commercial interests of the city.

Plate 84   Detail from William Mayo's map of Barbados. Engraved by John Senex, 1722. Reduced
to about half-size. The title cartouche is enriched with exuberant and gaily coloured naturalistic detail. In the vignette is seen the colonial surveyor using plane-table and chain, while one of his negro assistants holds a 'wheel dimensurator'. On the map, parishes are distinguished by contrasting colours and the names of landowners are given. Houses, mills and other buildings are in profile, as on Ogilby's map (Pl. 69).

NOMINAL INDEX

SUBJECT INDEX

PLATE I

Western Germany, from the 'Quarta Tabula Europae' in Ptolemy's *Geographia* (Rome, 1478)

PLATE 2

The World, in Ptolemy's *Geographia* (Ulm, 1482)

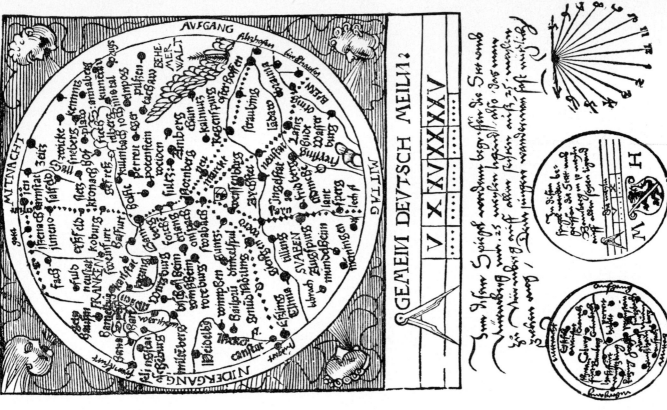

German road map of the environs of Nuremberg, early 15th century

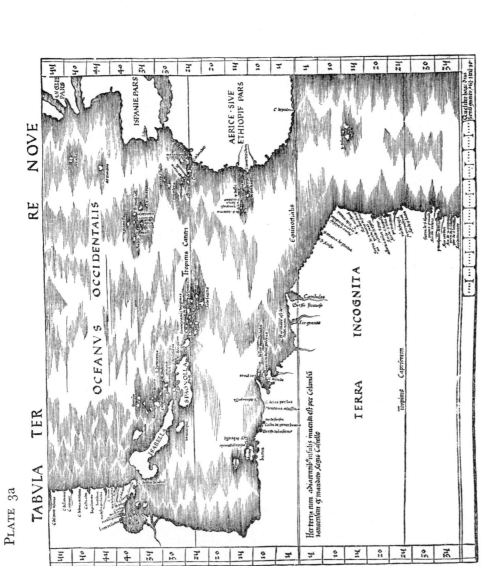

'Tabula Terre Nove', in Ptolemy's *Geographia* (Strassburg, 1513)

PLATE 4

INDIA EXTRA GANGEM

INDIA INTRA GANGEM

Sinus persicus

CARMANIA

ARABIE PARS

AFRICE PARS

SINVS MAGNVS

SINVS GANGETICVS

EQVINOCTIVS

Milaria

30 60 90 120 140 180 240 240 270

'Indiae Tabula Moderna', in Ptolemy's *Geographia* (Strassburg, 1522)

PLATE 5

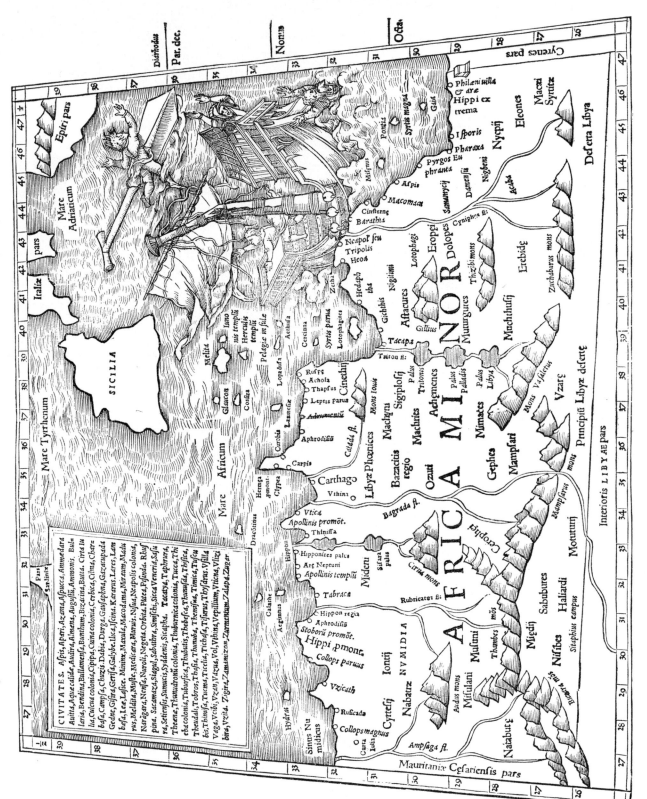

'Africa Minor', in Sebastian Münster's edition of Ptolemy (Basle, 1540)

PLATE 6

England, in Münster's edition of Ptolemy (Basle, 1540)

PLATE 7

The New World, in Münster's edition of Ptolemy (Basle, 1540)

PLATE 8

The World, in Peter Apian's *Cosmographia* edited by Gemma Frisius (Antwerp, 1545)

PLATE 9

Paris, in Sebastian Münster's *Cosmographia* (Basle, 1550)

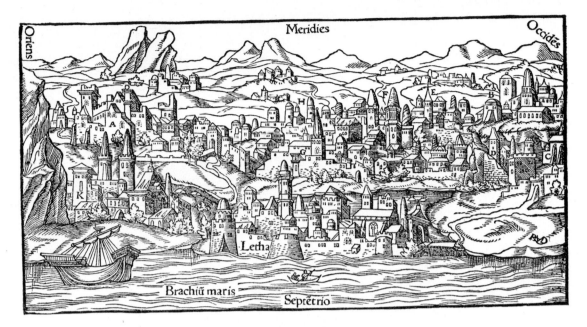

Edinburgh, in Münster's *Cosmographia* (Basle, 1550)

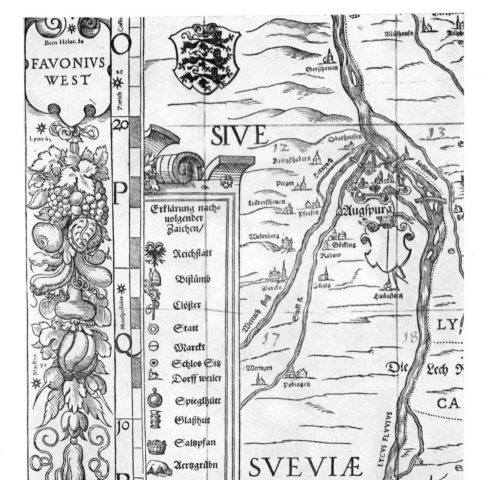

Detail of Philipp Apian's map of Bavaria,
Bairische Landtaflen XXIIII (Ingolstadt, 1568)

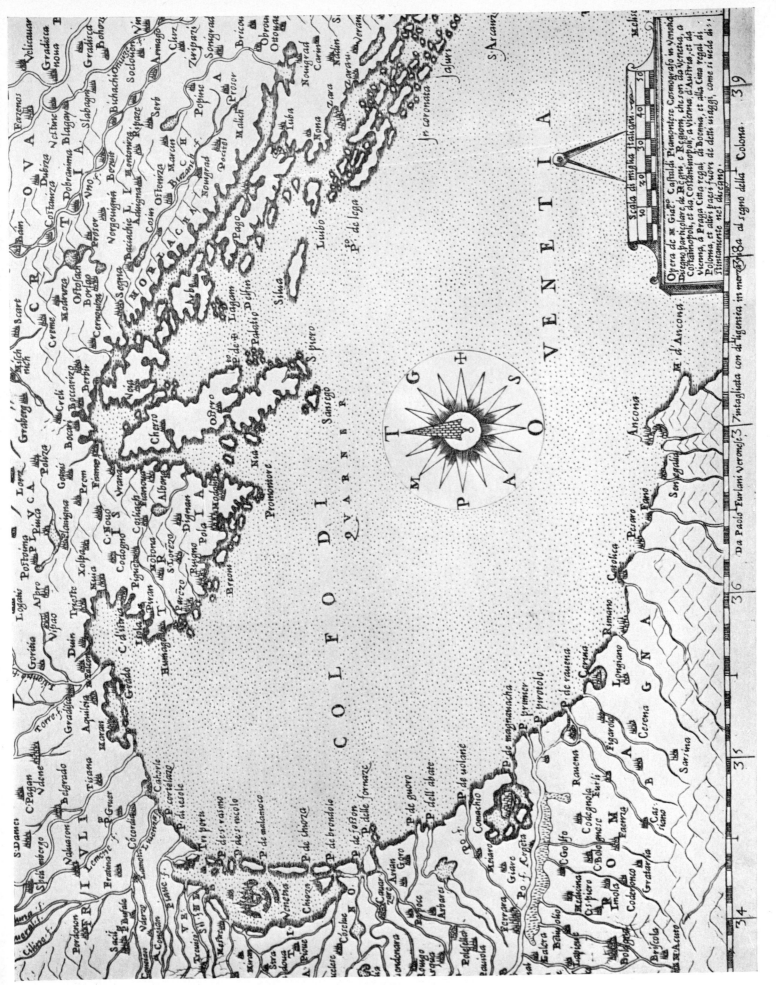

Detail of Jacopo Gastaldi's map of South-east Europe, 1566

PLATE 12

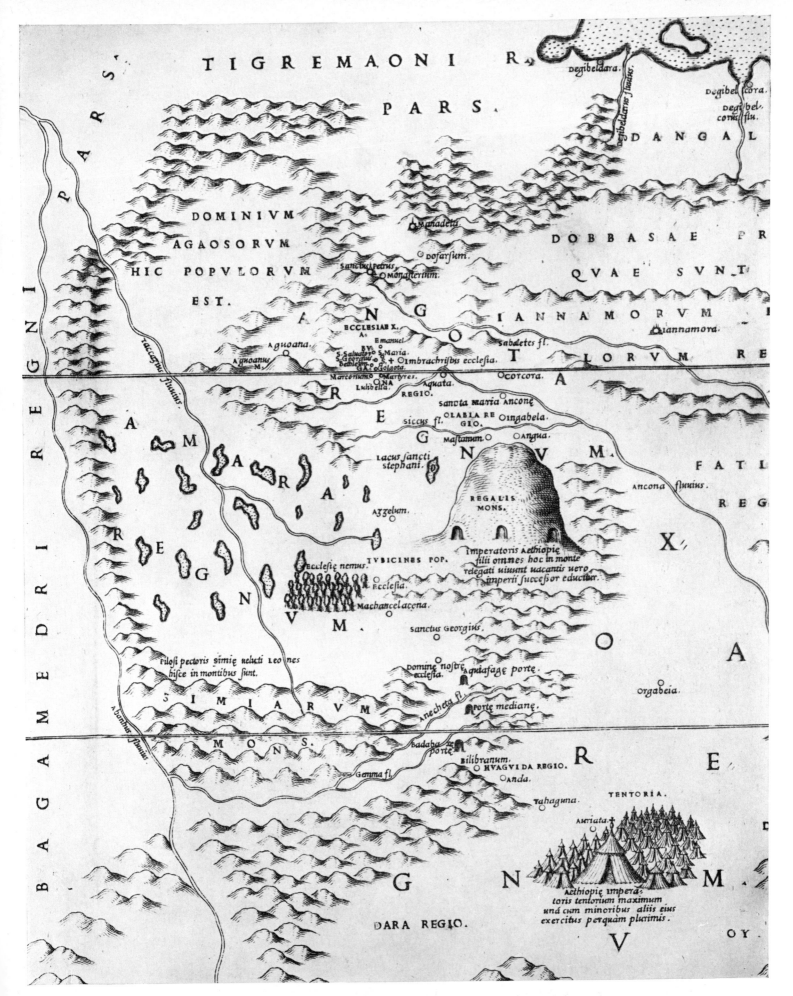

Abyssinia (detail of 'Africae Tabula VIIII'), in Livio Sanuto's *Geografia* (Venice, 1588)

PLATE 13

Detail of 'Asiae Tabula XI', in Mercator's edition of Ptolemy (Cologne, 1578)

PLATE 14

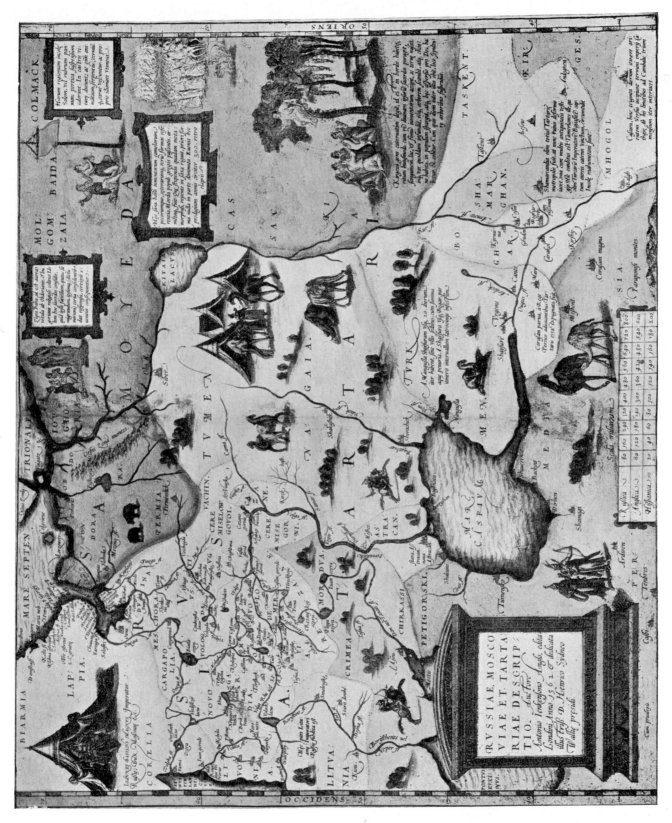

Russia, Muscovy and Tartary, in the *Theatrum orbis terrarum* of Abraham Ortelius (Antwerp, 1570)

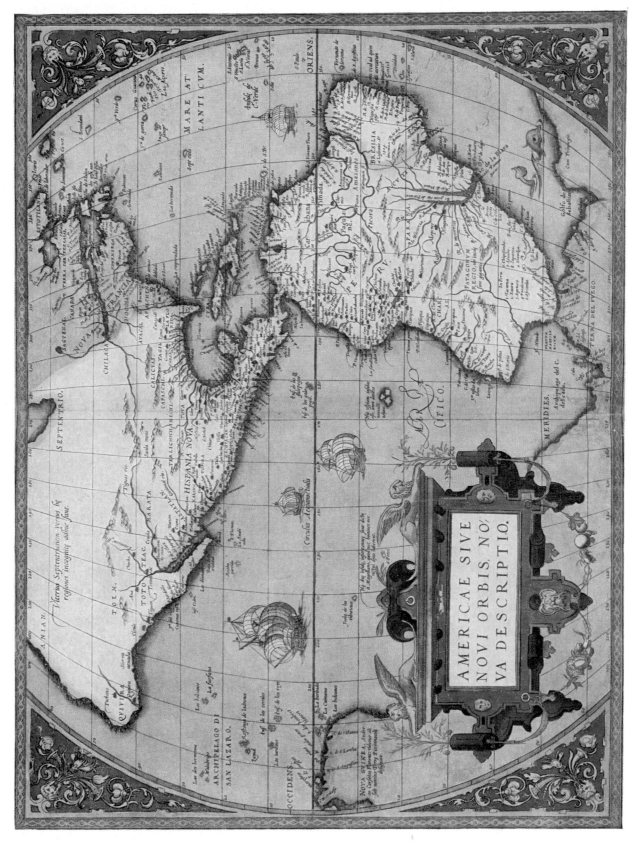

PLATE 15

The New World, 1587, in Ortelius's *Theatrum* (Antwerp, 1590)

PLATE 16

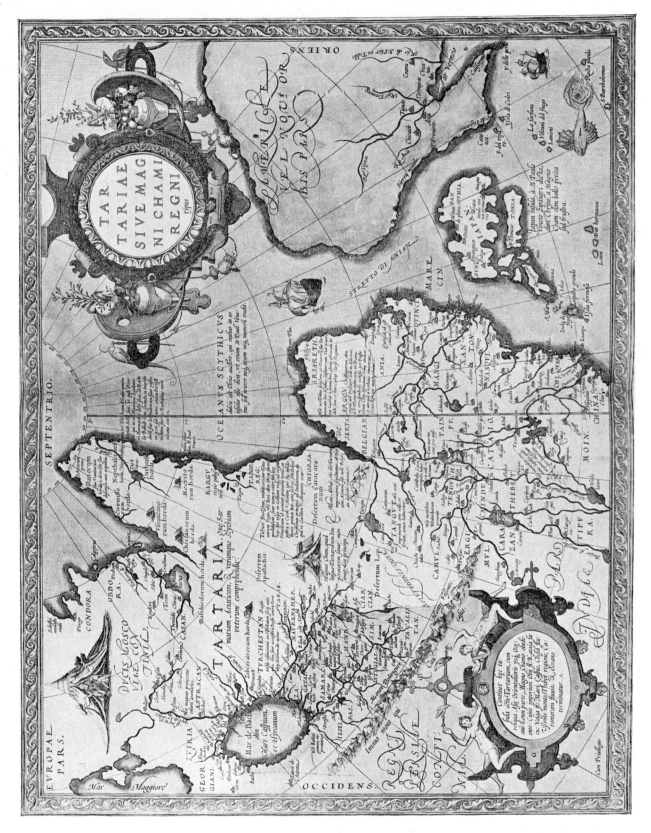

'Tartary, or the Kingdom of the Great Khan' in Ortelius's *Theatrum* (Antwerp, 1570)

PLATE 17

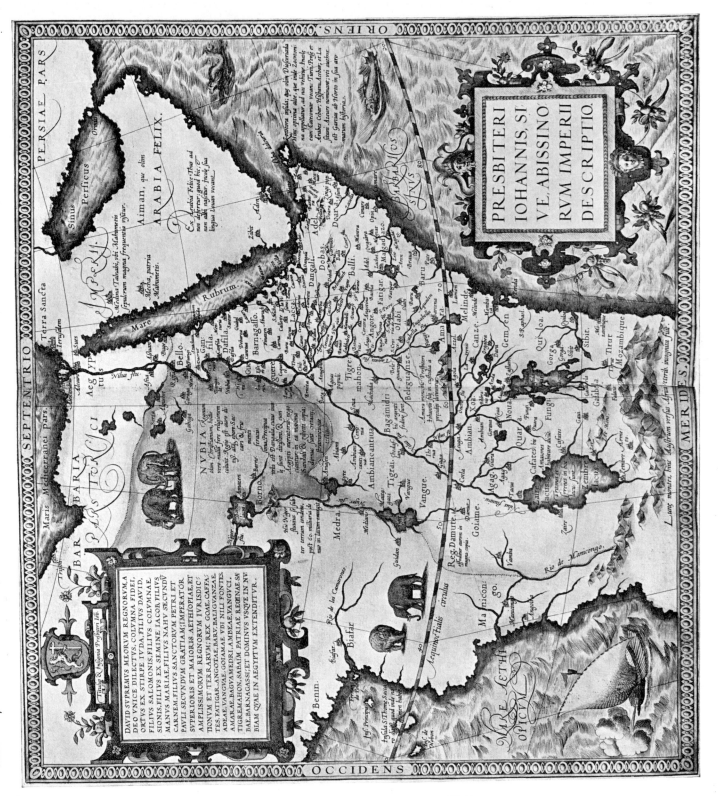

'The Empire of Prester John or of the Abyssinians', in Ortelius's *Theatrum* (Antwerp, 1573)

PLATE 18

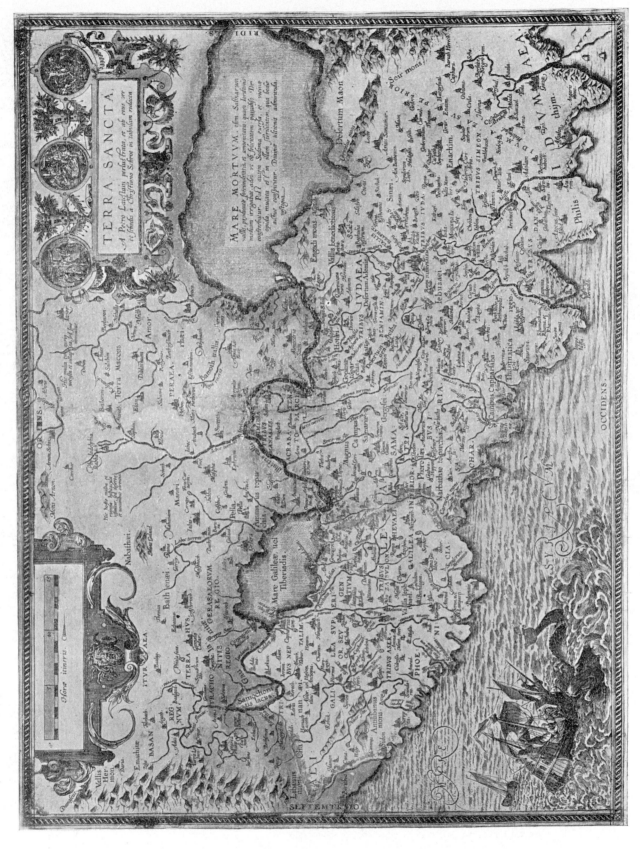

The Holy Land, in Ortelius's *Theatrum* (Antwerp, 1584)

PLATE 19

Byzantium or Constantinople, in the *Civitates orbis terrarum* of Georg Braun and Frans Hogenberg, vol. I (1573)

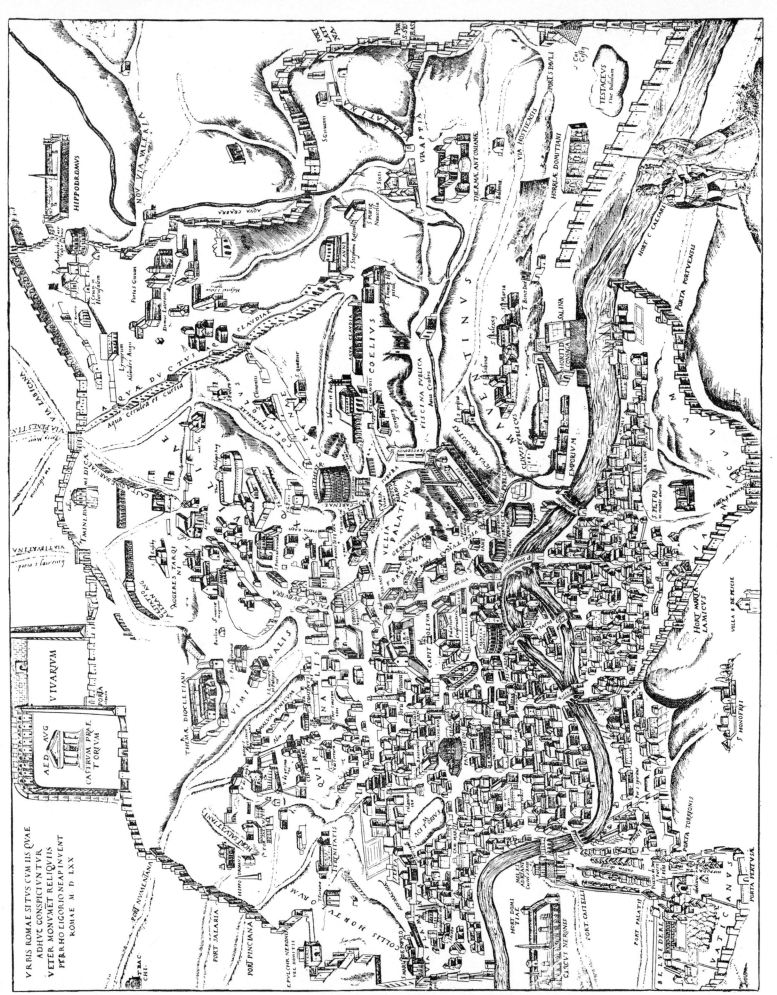

Rome and its monuments, in the *Civitates orbis terrarum*, vol. II (1575)

IERVSALEM

ORIENS

VAL Sepul LIS IOSA Cedro chra PHAT. 204 QVÆ

Torrens

SEPTENTRIO

Mons Caluariæ 233

Christ

Palatium Pilati
Palatium Herodis 137

Platea lata-

BEZETHA 147

NOVA CIVITAS 147

SECVNDA CIVITAS 125

Portæ Ephraim 151

FILIA SION QVÆ ET

Vivarium 144

Regia 152

Forum scrurarium 48

Mons OLI ue ti

Murus tertius 150

Murus Primus

Mons SION RA GI LIS VAL

OCCIDENS

Jerusalem, in the *Civitates orbis terrarum*, vol. IV (1588)

OSTENDA

PLATE 22

Ostend besieged by the Spaniards, 1601–4, in the *Civitates orbis terrarum*, vol. VI (1618)

PLATE 23

Title-page of *The Mariners Mirrour* by L. J. Waghenaer (London, 1588)

PLATE 24

The coasts of England from Scilly to Plymouth, in *The Mariners Mirrour* (London, 1588)

PLATE 25

Virginia, in Theodore de Bry's *America*, part I (Frankfort, 1590)

PLATE 26

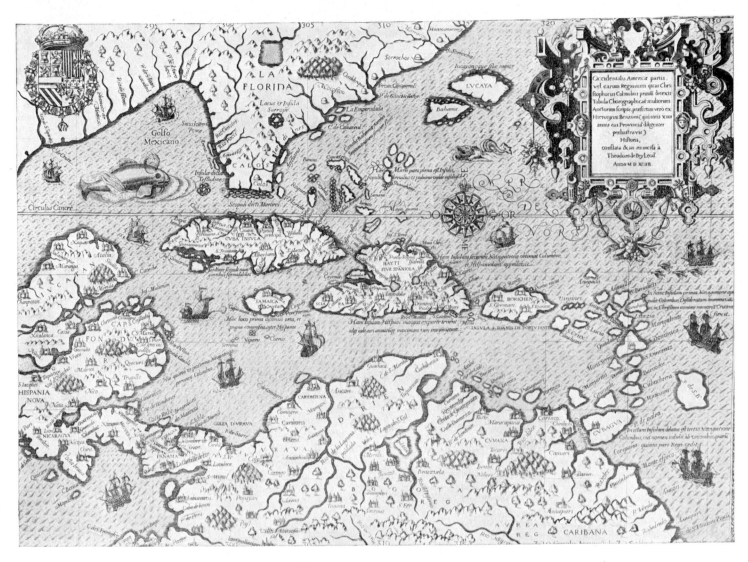

The West Indies, in Theodore de Bry's *America*, part IV (Frankfort, 1594)

PLATE 27

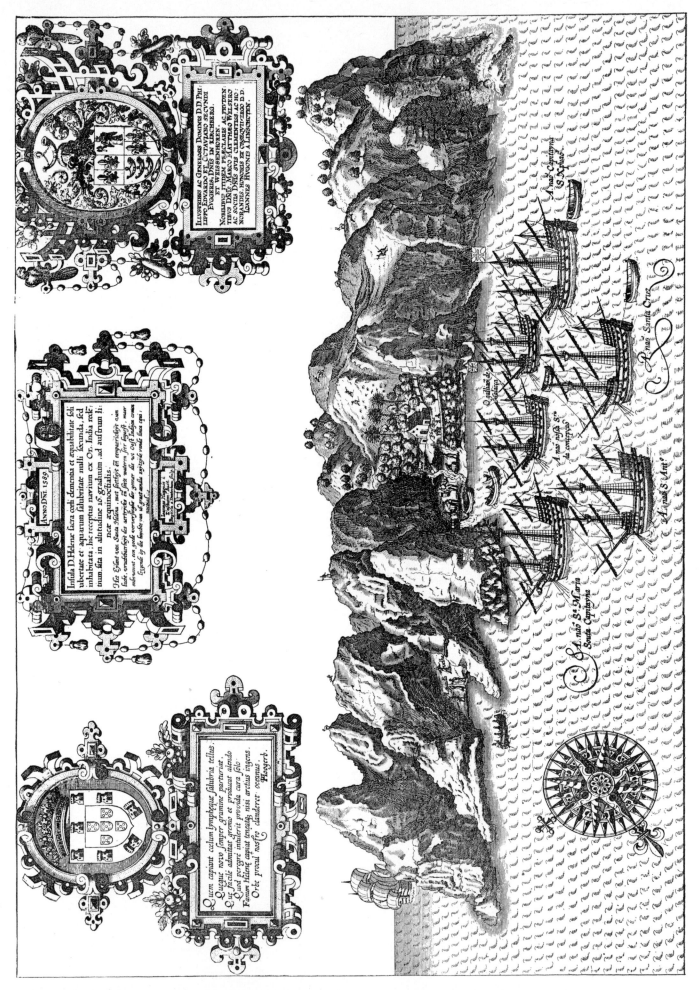

The Island of St Helena, engraved by Baptista van Deutecum, 1589. In J. H. van Linschoten's *Itinerario*.

Voyage ofte Schipvaert (Amsterdam, 1596)

PLATE 28

South America, engraved by Arnold van Langeren. In Linschoten's *Itinerario* (Amsterdam, 1596)

PLATE 29

The Indian Ocean, engraved by Hendrik van Langeren. In Linschoten's *Itinerario* (Amsterdam, 1596)

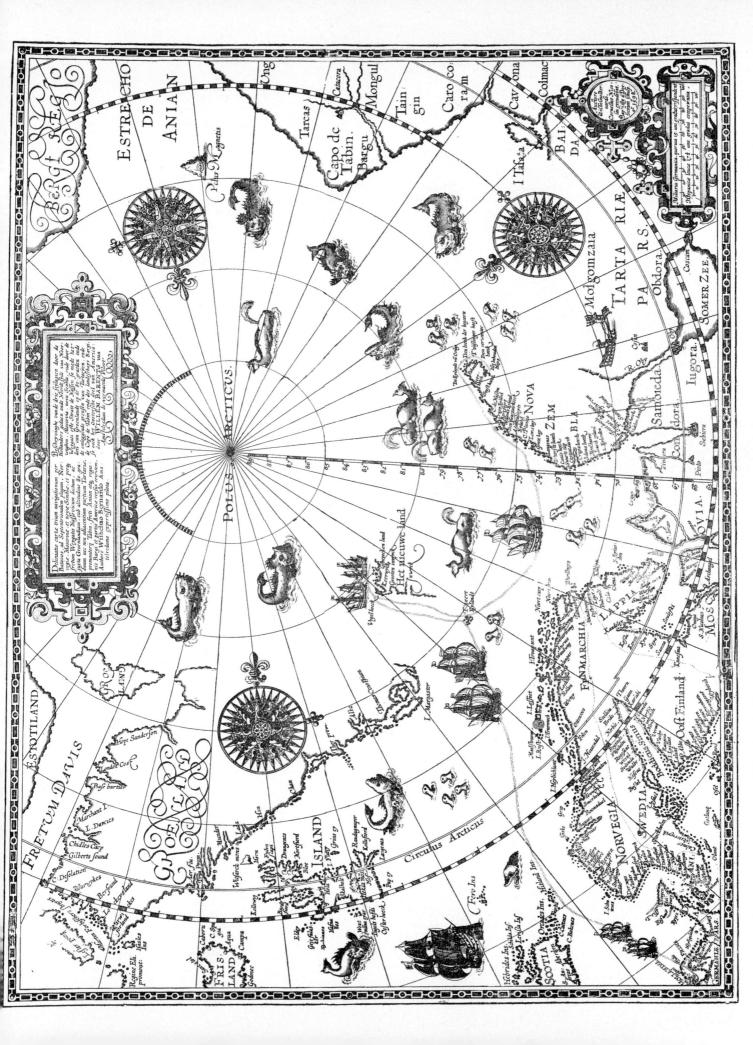

The Arctic Regions, by Willem Barents, engraved by Baptista van Deutecum, 1598.

In Linschoten's *Navigatio ac itinerarium* (The Hague, 1599)

PLATE 31

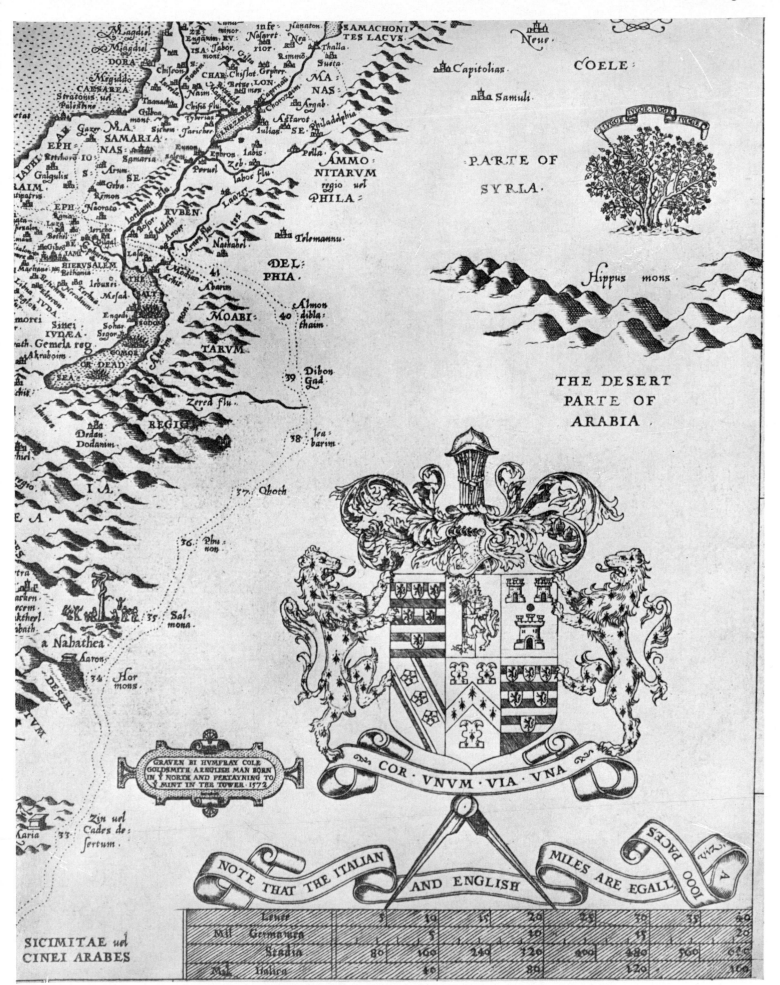

The Holy Land (detail), engraved by Humphry Cole, 1572

PLATE 32

Staffordshire, by Christopher Saxton. Engraved by Francis Scatter, 1577

PLATE 33

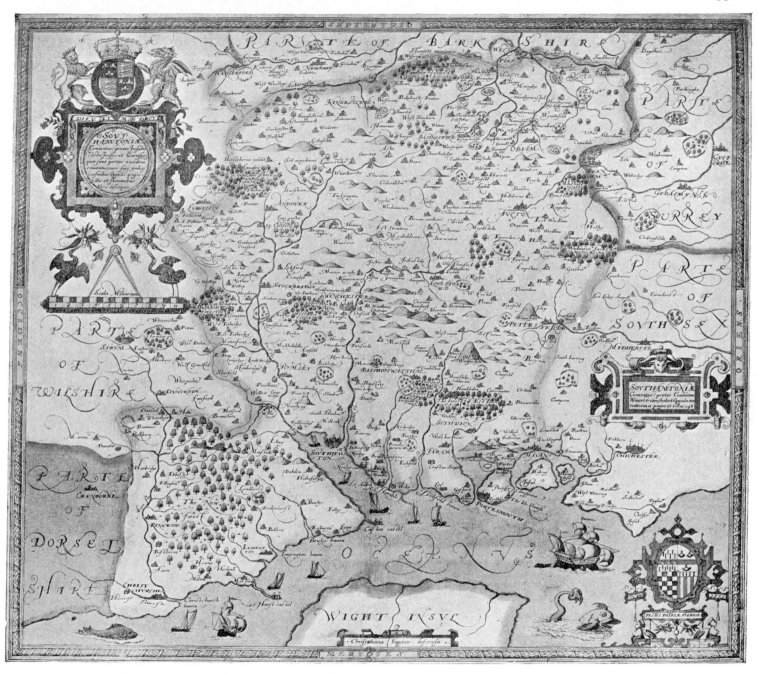

Hampshire, by Christopher Saxton. Engraved by Leonhart Terwoort, 1575

PLATE 34

Mediocria.

Parua.

*

Integra huius Scalæ Longitudo vni Latitudinis gradui respondet ∞

Parallelus 50 graduum Latitudinis Borealis.

The Gulfe

Scoringes Insula.

Longitudinis gradus ab eo Meridiano capiunt
initium qui per duas Mariæ Insulæ transit quæ
omnium Azoreæ, maxime ad Orientem vergit

16   17   XVII   18

50   51

Cornwall and the Scilly Isles: Plate XVII of Saxton's large map of England and Wales, 1583

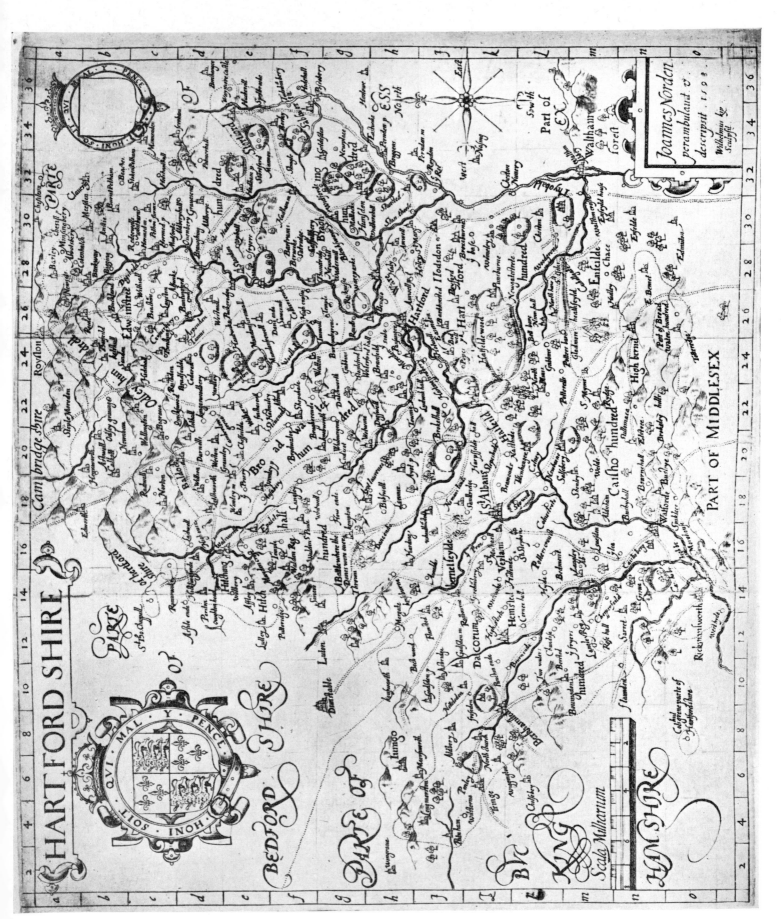

Hertfordshire, by John Norden. Engraved by William Kip in Norden's *Speculi Britanniae pars.*

The description of Hartfordshire (London, 1598)

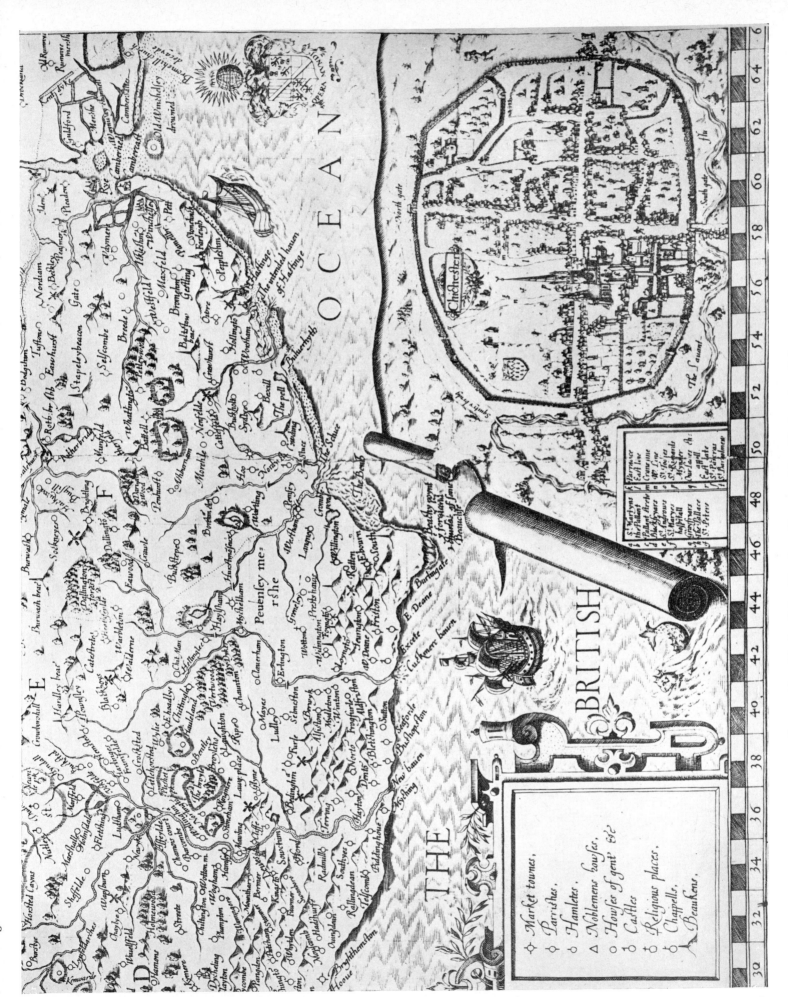

Sussex (detail), by John Norden. Engraved by Christopher Schwytzer, 1595

Anglo-Saxon Britain, in John Speed's *Theatre of the Empire of Great Britaine* (London, 1611–12)

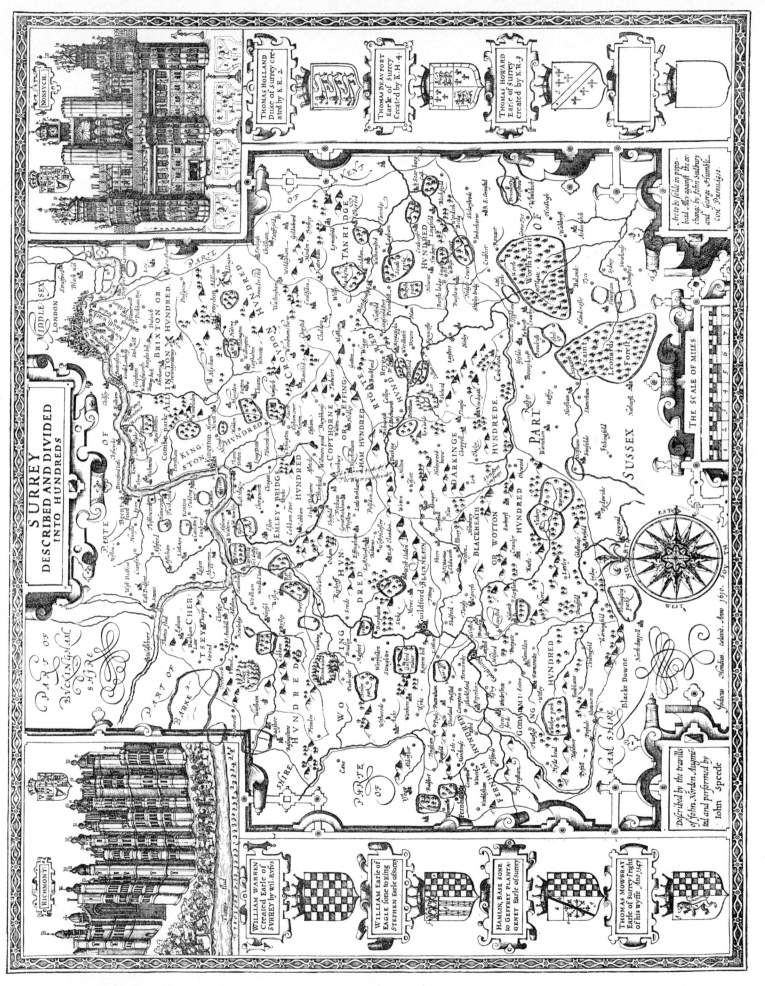

Surrey, in Speed's *Theatre* (London, 1611-12)

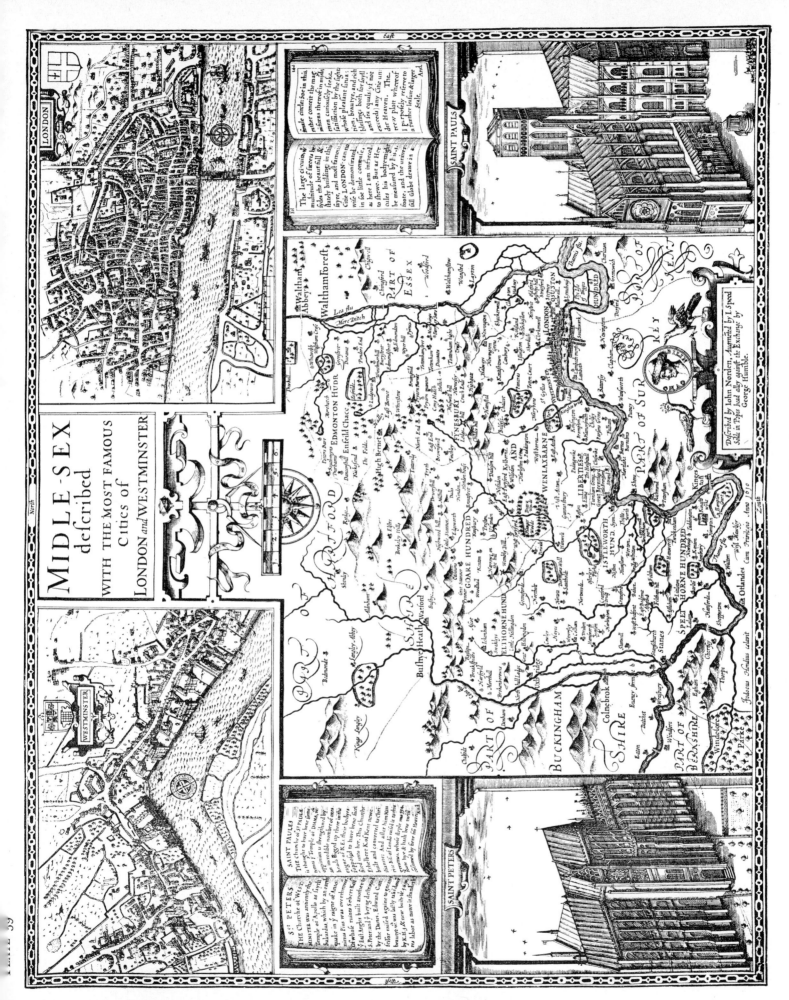

Middlesex, in Speed's *Theatre* (London, 1611–12)

PLATE 40

Cambridgeshire, in Speed's *Theatre* (London, 1611–12)

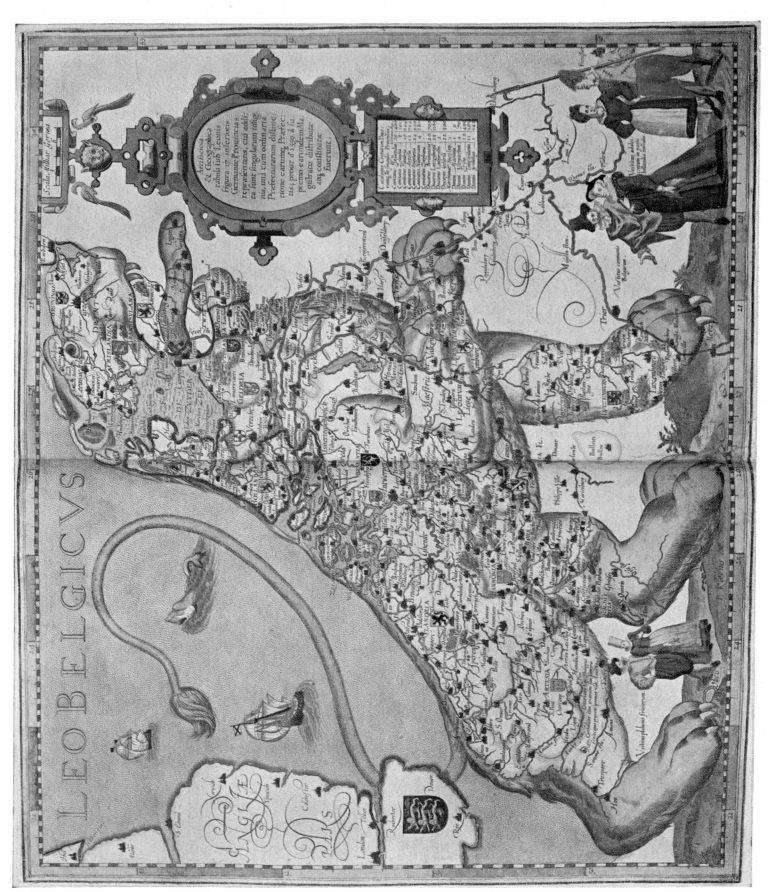

The Seventeen Provinces of the United Netherlands, engraved by Pieter van den Keere in *Germania Inferior* (Amsterdam, 1617)

Detail of 'Territorio di Bergamo', in G. A. Magini's *Italia* (Bologna, 1620)

PLATE 43

Fez and Morocco, in the Mercator-Hondius *Atlas* (Amsterdam, 1606)

China, in the Mercator-Hondius *Atlas* (Amsterdam, 1606)

Japan, in the Mercator-Hondius *Atlas* (Amsterdam, 1606)

PLATE 45

PLATE 46

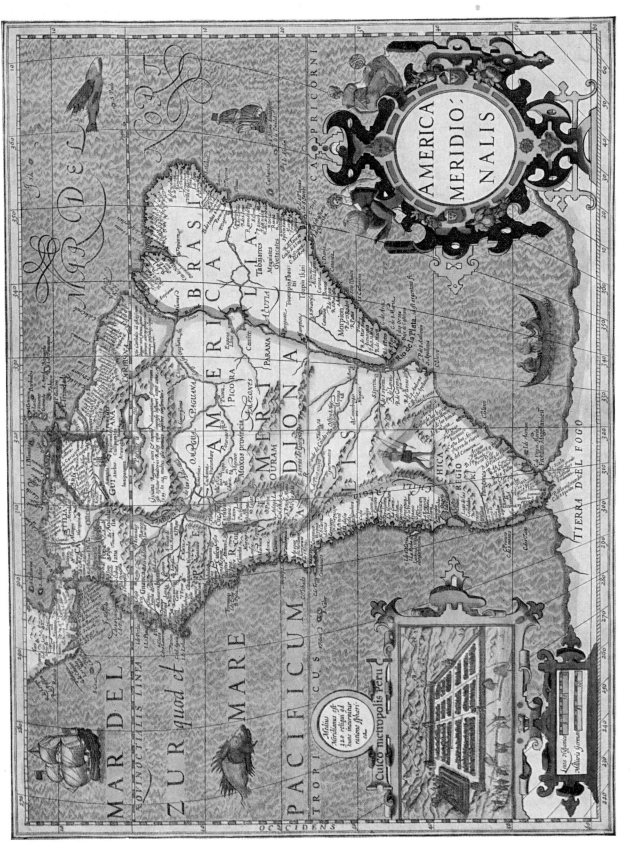

South America, in the Mercator-Hondius *Atlas* (Amsterdam, 1606)

PLATE 47

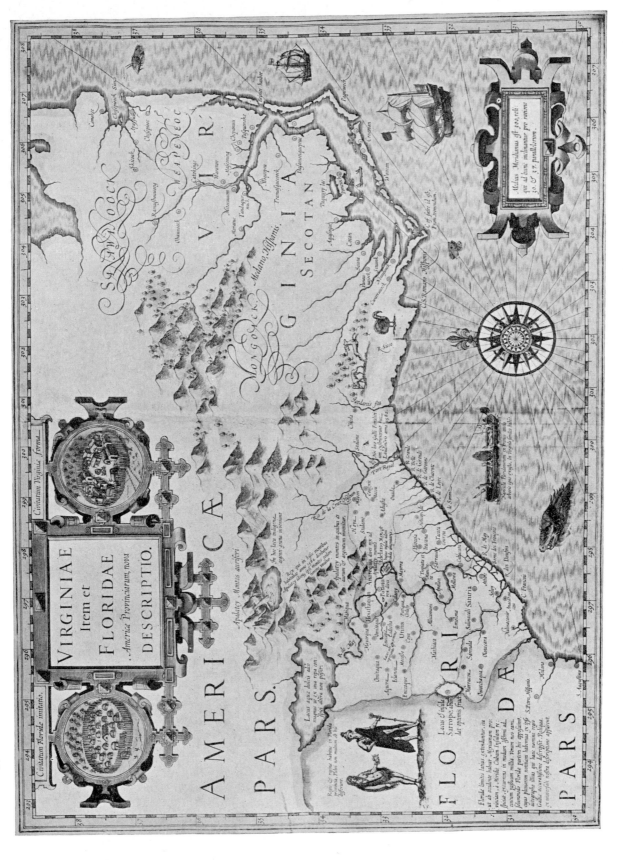

Virginia and Florida, in the Mercator-Hondius *Atlas* (Amsterdam, 1606)

PLATE 48

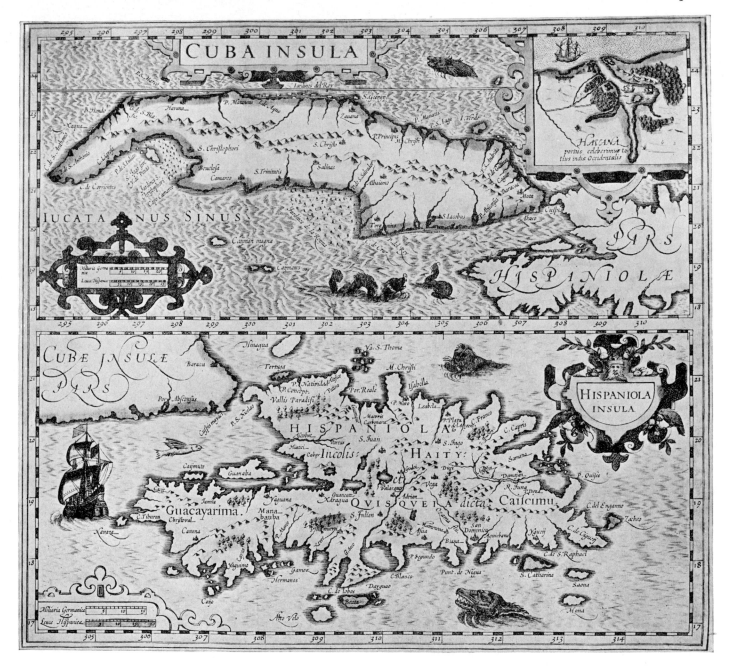

Cuba and Hispaniola, in the Mercator-Hondius *Atlas* (Amsterdam, 1606)

PLATE 49

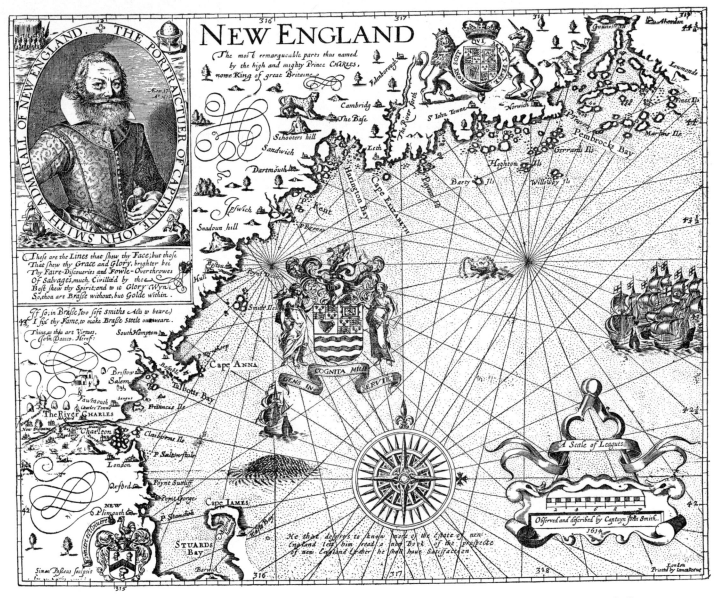

New England, by Captain John Smith, 1614. Engraved by Simon van de Passe, c. 1616

PLATE 50

Virginia, engraved by Ralph Hall, 1636

PLATE 51

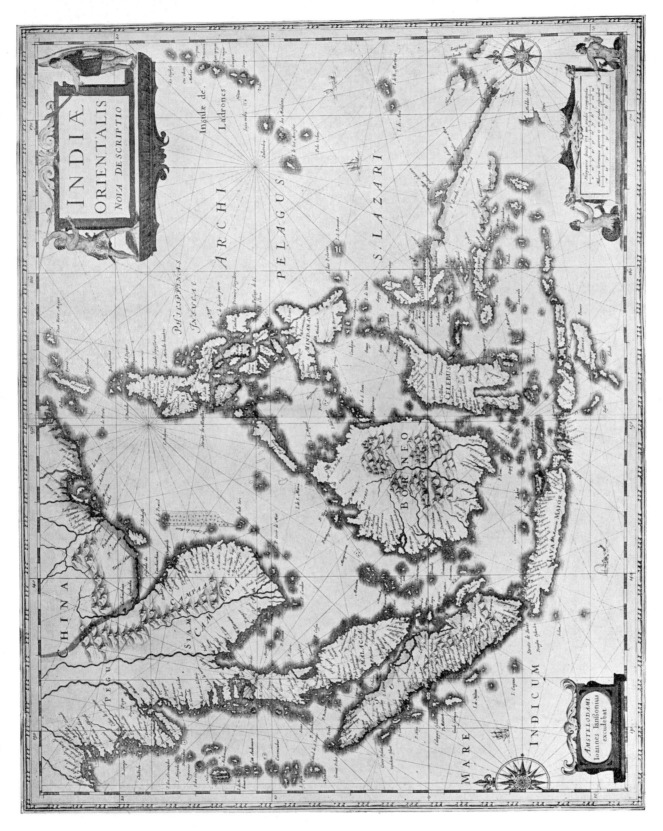

The East Indies, in the Mercator-Hondius *Atlas* (Amsterdam, 1633)

PLATE 52

Essex, in the *Novus Atlas* of Jan Jansson, vol. IV (Amsterdam, 1646)

PLATE 53

Title-page of Jansson's *Novus Atlas*, vol. IV, German edition (Amsterdam, 1647)

Plate 55

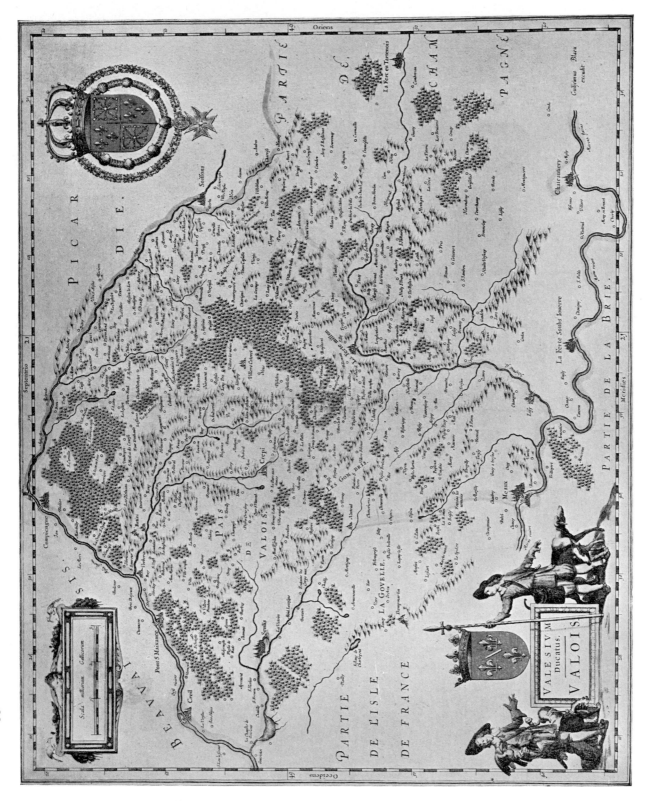

Valois, in W. J. Blaeu's *Novus Atlas* (Amsterdam, 1635), vol. I

PLATE 56

America, in Blaeu's *Novus Atlas* (Amsterdam, 1635), vol. I

PLATE 57

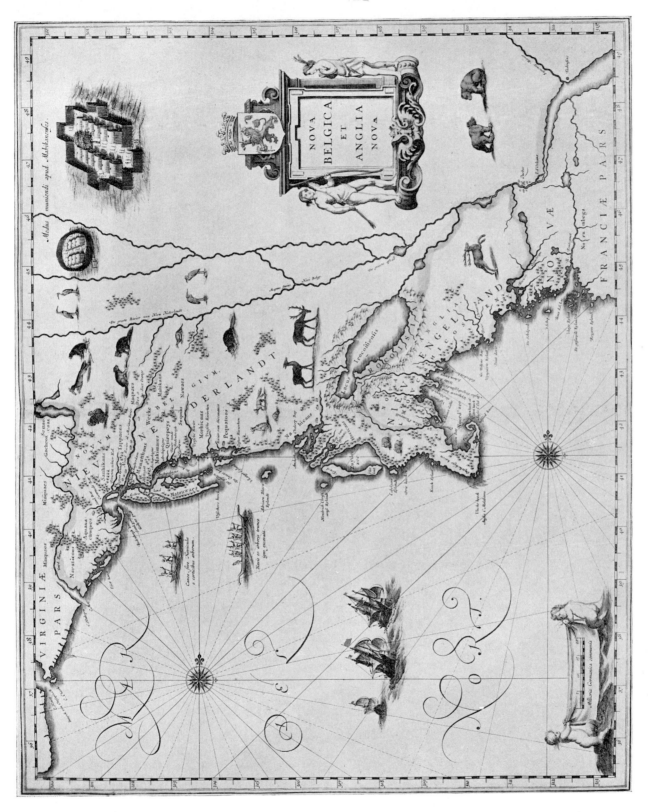

New Belgium and New England, in Blaeu's *Novus Atlas* (Amsterdam, 1635), vol. II

PLATE 58

Brazil, in Blaeu's *Novus Atlas* (Amsterdam, 1635), vol. II

PLATE 59

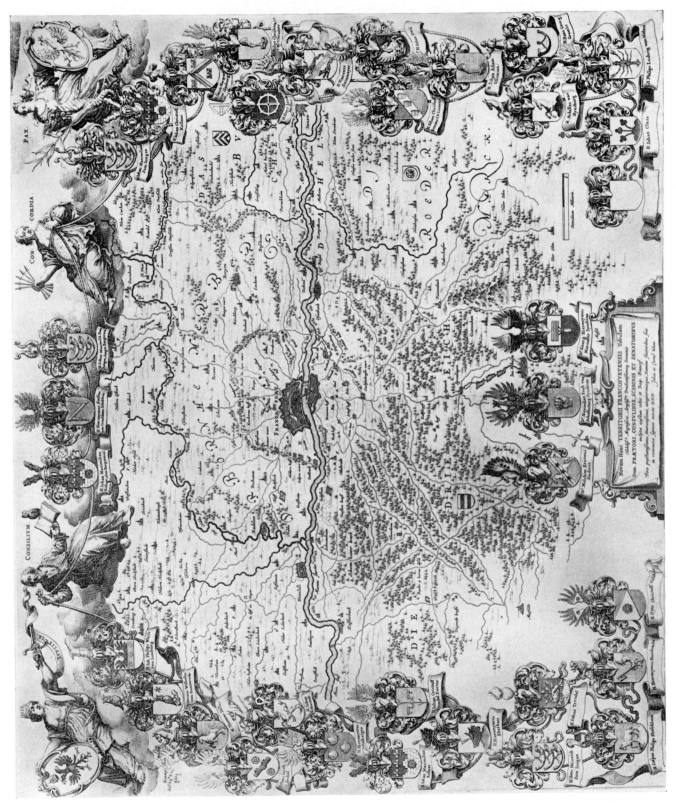

The Territory of Frankfort, in Blaeu's *Novus Atlas* (Amsterdam, 1640), vol. I

PLATE 60

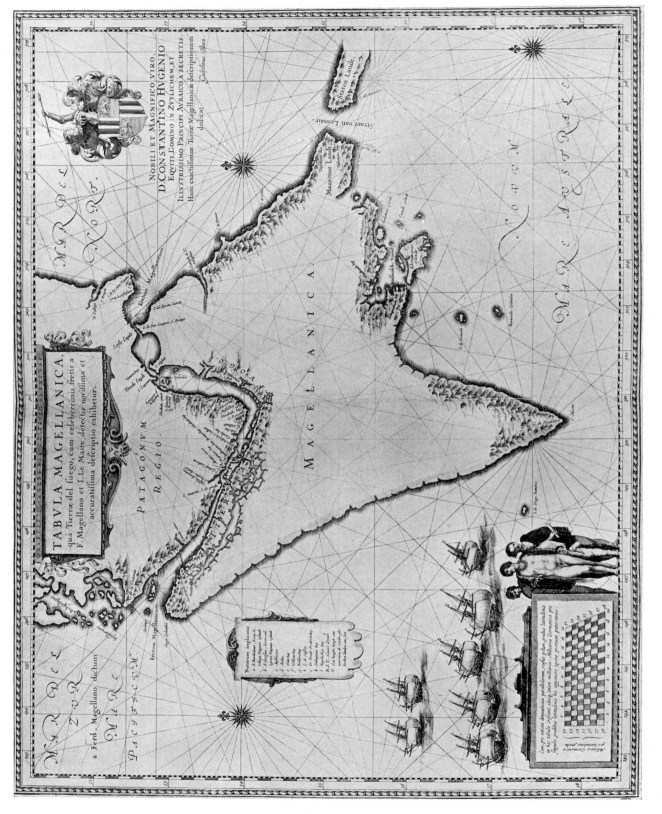

Tierra del Fuego and the Magellan Strait, in Blaeu's *Novus Atlas* (Amsterdam, 1640), vol. II

PLATE 61

ARANIA
Insula in aestuario Glottæ
THE YLE OF ARREN
in the Fyrth of Clyd

Scala Milliarium

Oriens

Occidens

Meridies

Septentrio

Vulgo

Part of Knapdail

Loch Terbert

Part of Kintyr

The Isle of Arran, in Blaeu's *Atlas Novus*, vol. V (Amsterdam, 1654)

PLATE 62

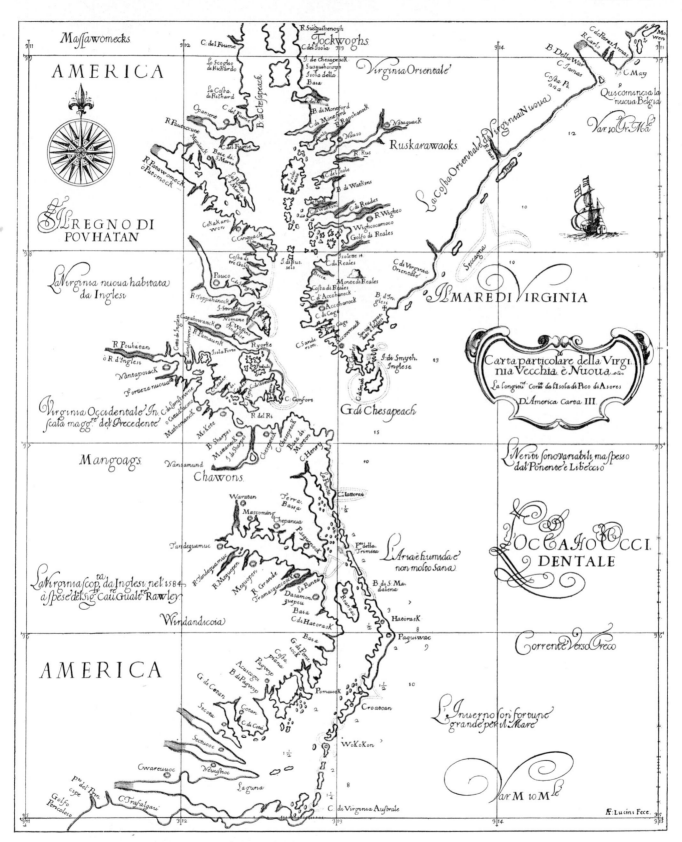

'Old and New Virginia', in Sir Robert Dudley's *Dell' Arcano del Mare* (Florence, 1646–47), book VI

PLATE 63

Guiana, in Dudley's *Dell' Arcano del Mare* (Florence, 1646–47), book VI

PLATE 64

Title-page of *De Zee-atlas,* by Pieter Goos (Amsterdam, 1666)

PLATE 65

Chart of the North Sea (detail) in *De Zee-atlas* of Pieter Goos (Amsterdam, 1675)

PLATE 66

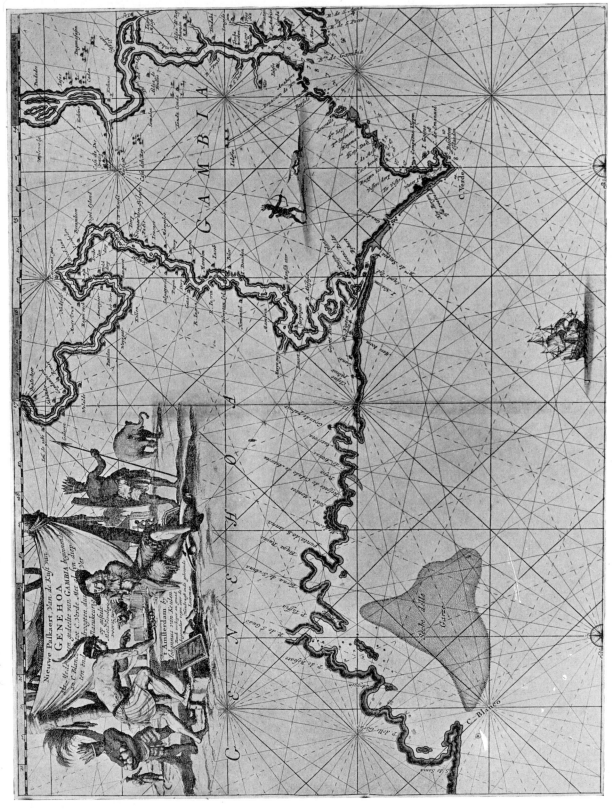

The Coast of Guinea, in *De Zee-atlas* of J. van Keulen (Amsterdam, 1681)

PLATE 67

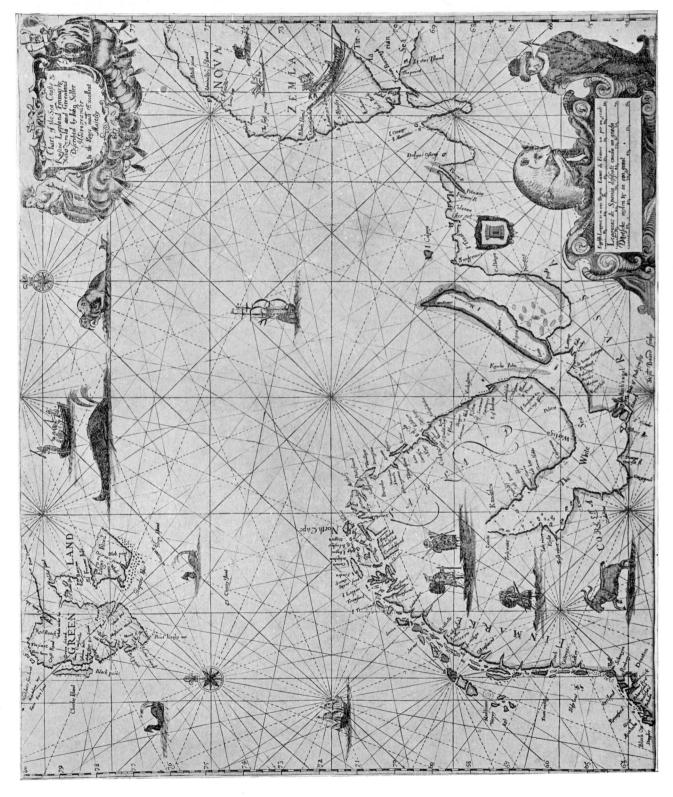

The Coasts of Northern Europe, by John Seller, in *The English Pilot*, book I (London, 1671)

Chart of Dartmouth, with inset of Torbay. In *Great Britain's Coasting Pilot*, by Captain Greenvile Collins (London, 1693)

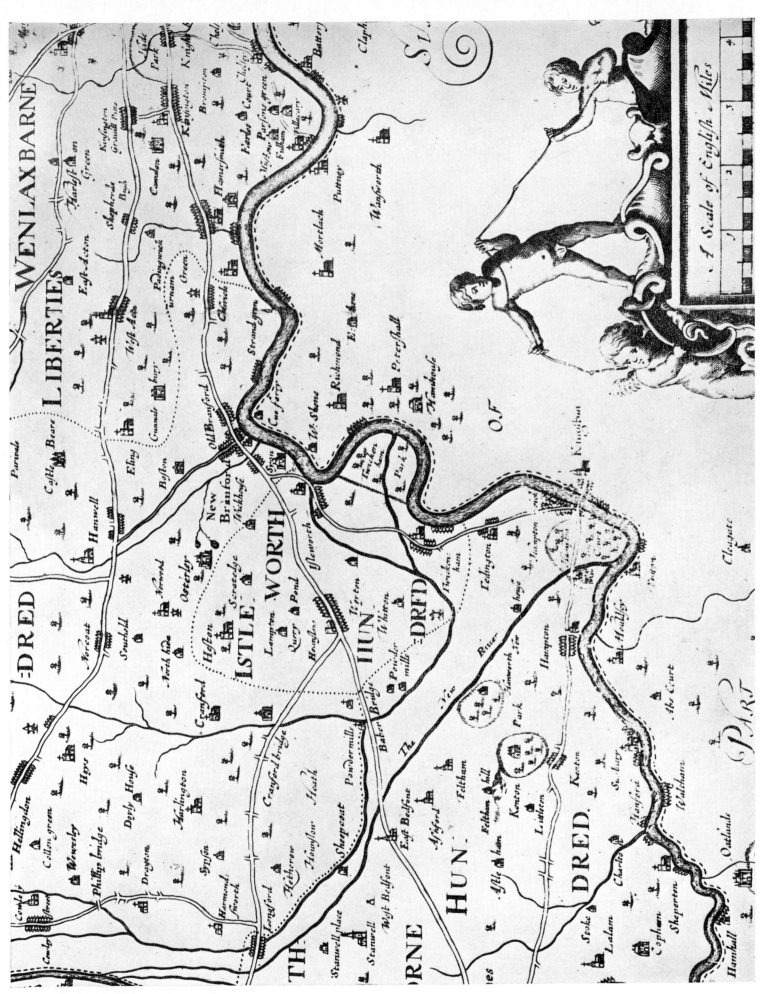

Middlesex (detail), by John Ogilby. Engraved by Walter Binneman, c. 1677

PLATE 70

...GNO DI NEGROPONTE

...everendis.mo P. Maestro Felice Rotondi
Teologo Publico nell'Università
di Padoua

ARCIPELAGO

ISOLA, e REGNO DI NEGROPONTE

STRETTO DI NEGROPONTE

ARCIPELAGO

MARE

Mare Caphararuni

ACHAIA

PUS EUBOICUS.

GOLFO D'ENGIA

EGEO

LO STRETTO

ISOLA

Città

Castello

PARTE DELL'
ACHAIA

Forte
Carababa,

Borgo

NEGROPONTE DI

DI NEGROPONTE

MELIORA LEONI

Negroponte, by V. M. Coronelli (Venice, c. 1690)

PLATE 71

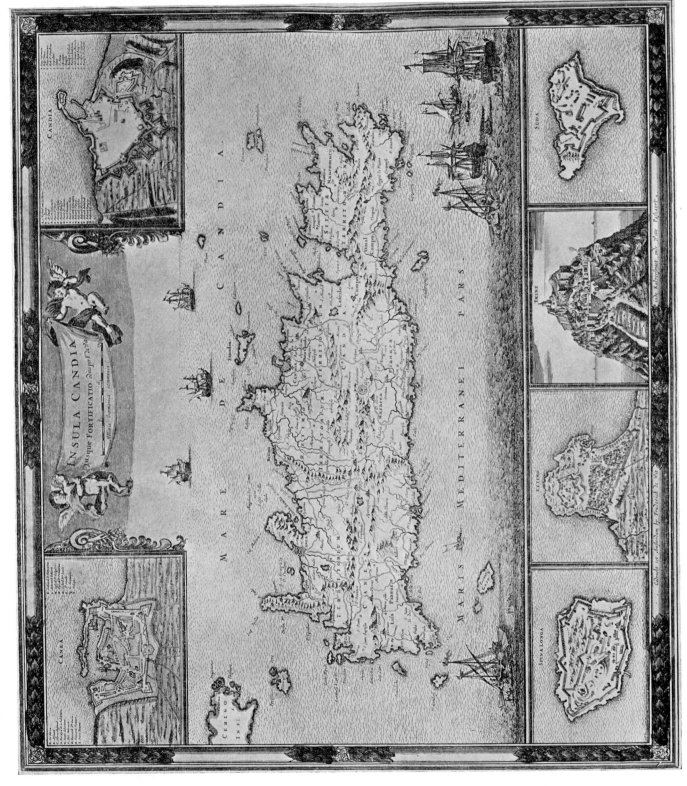

Candia (Crete), by Frederik de Wit (Amsterdam, c. 1680)

Star chart of the Southern Hemisphere, calculated for the year 1700. By Karel Allard, Amsterdam

PLATE 73

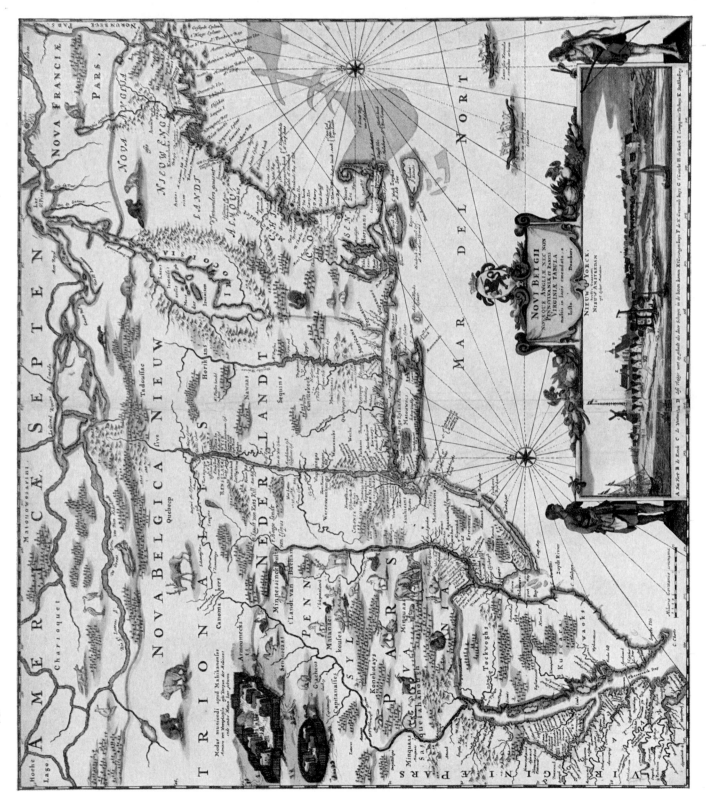

New Belgium, New England, Virginia, with inset view of New York. By Justus Danckerts, Amsterdam, *post* 1683

PLATE 74

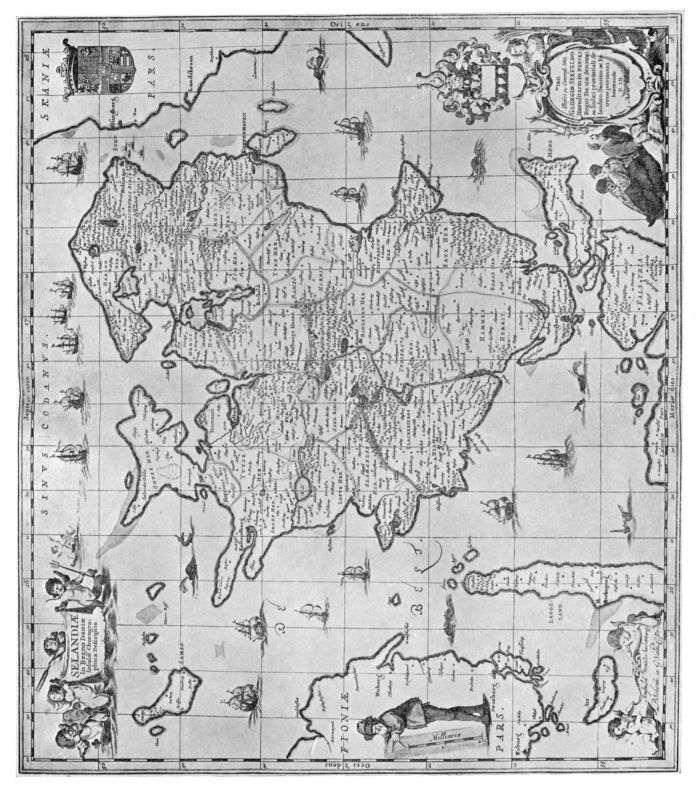

Zealand (Denmark), in Pieter Schenk's *Atlas Contractus* (Amsterdam, *post* 1713)

PLATE 75

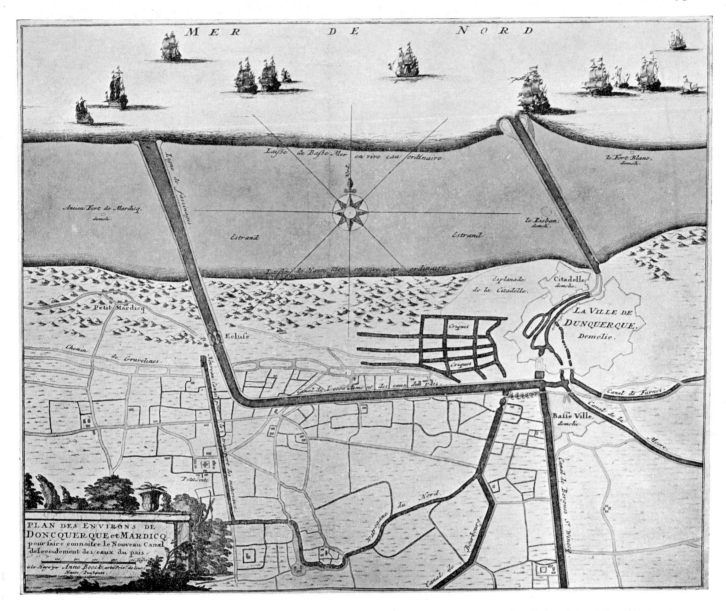

Dunkirk and Mardyck, published by Anne Beeck, The Hague, *post* 1713. In Schenk's *Atlas Contractus*

PLATE 76

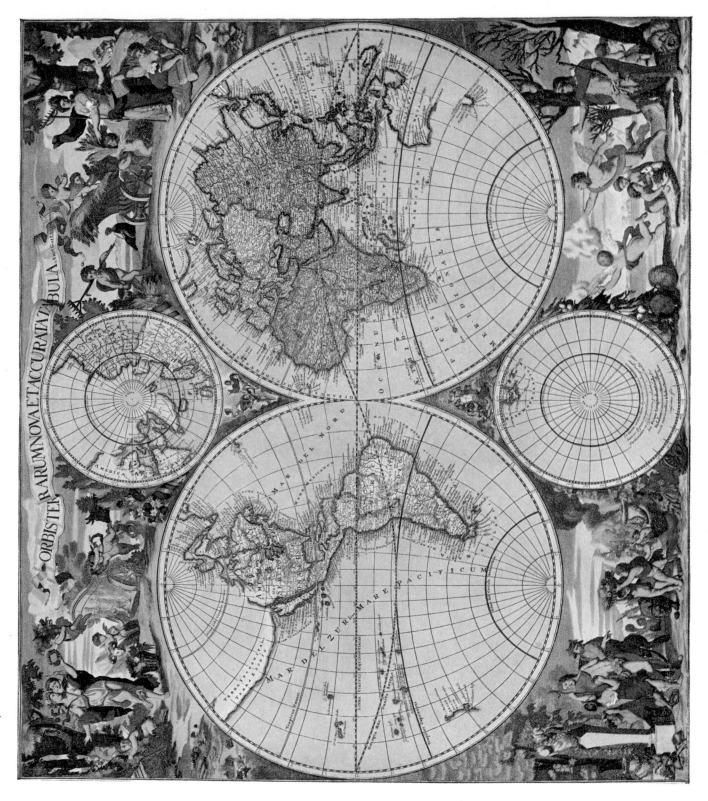

The World, by Gerard and Leonard Valk, Amsterdam, c. 1690. In Schenk's *Atlas Contractus*

PLATE 78

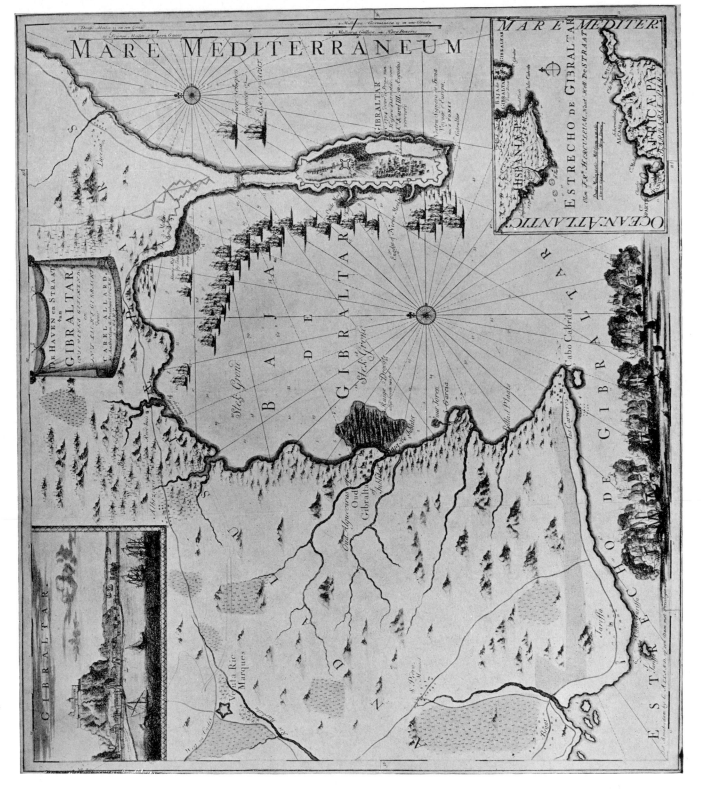

Gibraltar, published by Karel Allard, Amsterdam, *post* 1704. In Schenk's *Atlas Contractus*

PLATE 79

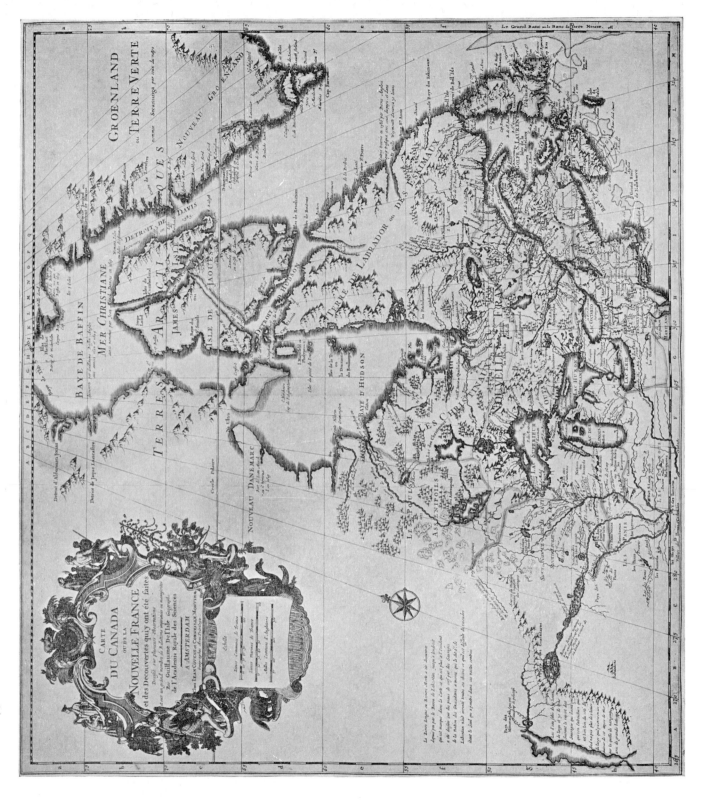

Canada, by Guillaume Delisle (Paris, 1703)

PLATE 80

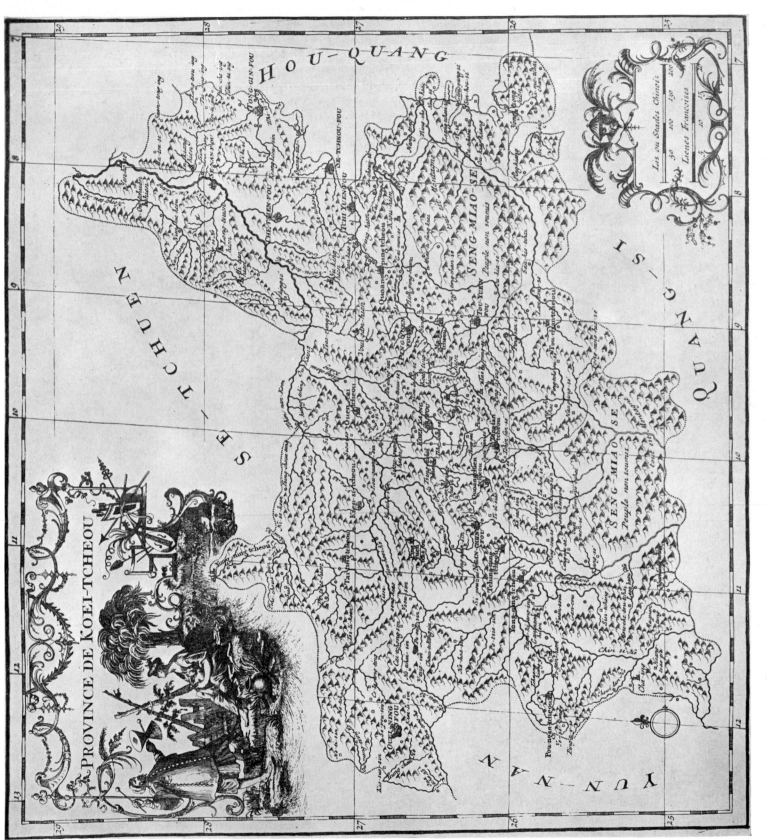

The Province of Kwei-chow, in J. B. Bourguignon d'Anville's *Nouvel Atlas de la Chine* (The Hague, 1737)

PLATE 81

Detail from *Atlas topographique des environs de Paris*, by Cassini (Paris, 1768)

PLATE 62

The Five Field

KNIGHTS BR

Tyburn

Marylebo

PARK

The Serpentine River

the King's Old Road

the King's New Road

Gore

Kensington

Hogmore

Love Lane

Brick Kiln

Royal Palace and Garden

The Bason

KENSINGTON

Court Lane

Hell House

Lane

West

Court Lane

Kensington, from John Rocque's *Survey of London and Westminster and the country . . . round* (London, 1746)